THE THINKING OFFICER'S GUIDE
TO POLICE DEFENSIVE TACTICS

ABOUT THE AUTHOR

Perry William Kelly is a lawyer who works as a senior policy advisor in the police and law enforcement directorate of the Solicitor General of Canada. A former correctional investigator and Assistant Director of Operations for the Royal Canadian Mounted Police Public Complaints Commission, he is also a longtime practitioner and instructor of a wide variety of martial arts. His legal education, martial arts training, and experience in the criminal justice system have given him a unique ability to understand the mentality and techniques utilized by today's criminal element. As a certified police defensive tactics instructor, he also possesses an in-depth understanding of the techniques that are of foremost importance to today's law enforcement agencies. His knowledge of the history, evolution, and intellectual framework of the various fighting systems results in a unique, yet realistic and practical approach to self-defense training. For the past ten years, he has been a featured writer in the *RCMP Gazette* and other police publications on the subjects of police defensive tactics and officer survival.

THE THINKING OFFICER'S GUIDE TO POLICE DEFENSIVE TACTICS

By

PERRY WILLIAM KELLY

With a Foreword by

Norman Inkster

CHARLES C THOMAS • PUBLISHER, LTD.
Springfield • Illinois • U.S.A.

Published and Distributed Throughout the World by

CHARLES C THOMAS • PUBLISHER, LTD.
2600 South First Street
Springfield, Illinois 62794-9265

© *1998 by* CHARLES C THOMAS • PUBLISHER, LTD.
ISBN 0-398-06862-3 (cloth)
ISBN 0-398-06863-1 (paper)

Library of Congress Catalog Card Number: 98-11101

With THOMAS BOOKS *careful attention is given to all details of manufacturing
and design. It is the Publisher's desire to present books that are satisfactory as to their
physical qualities and artistic possibilities and appropriate for their particular use.*
THOMAS BOOKS *will be true to those laws of quality that assure a good name
and good will.*

Printed in the United States of America
CR-R-3

Library of Congress Cataloging in Publication Data
Kelly, Perry William.
    The thinking officer's guide to police defensive tactics / by
Perry William Kelly : with a foreword by Norman Inkster.
        p.   cm.
    Includes bibliographical references and index.
    ISBN 0-398-06862-3 (cloth). -- ISBN 0-398-06869-1 (paper)
    1. Police patrol. 2. Self-defense. 3. Martial arts. I. Title.
HV8080.P2K44   1998
363.2'32--dc21   98-11101
                                                           CIP

*This book is dedicated to my daughter Sydney-Quinn,
with the hope that she will see the day
that the information it contains is used for historical
purposes only.*

FOREWORD

Our world is no longer as safe as it once was, and the police to whom we often turn for assistance need to be prepared for situations where they must protect themselves and others, but use no more force than is absolutely necessary in doing so. Others feel the need to be able to better protect themselves.

The cinema and the media keep these concerns present in our minds. Countless movies, television dramas and popular books have provided us with incredibly exciting and dynamic fight scenes. However, the true art of martial arts and self-defense are far from easy. As readers of this book will discover, training in the martial arts and self-defense are not talents to be taken for granted. They, in fact, require great skill, intellect, and continued practice for a truly enlightened understanding of the art of self-defense.

In *The Thinking Officer's Guide to Police Defensive Tactics,* Mr. Kelly introduces an innovative method of presenting and learning defensive tactics from a book. Mr. Kelly draws heavily on his life experience, legal education and martial arts training and on the insights he has developed by working in these fields. His realistic approach to self-defense training provides readers with an historical and intellectual overview of the various forms of fighting systems, such as Filipino Martial Arts, Jeet Kune Do, street fighting and Silat, and offers clear, concise explanations of many different styles of fighting and self-defense. By presenting the reader with anecdotal evidence, including information obtained from prison inmates and medical authorities about their ideas on fighting and self-defense, Mr. Kelly informs us about the reality of what the police are really up against out there "on the beat." Knowledge is key to the art of fighting and Mr. Kelly successfully links ancient traditions to modern police forces. He offers several recommendations to police forces on the art of self-defense, including an emphasis on the continual training of self-defense techniques throughout one's police service.

The author is appropriately concerned about the need for a full understanding of the balance required between the mental and physical components, as well as the essential application of both in the use, not misuse, of these extraordinary skills.

NORMAN D. INKSTER

President of KPMG Investigation and Security Inc.
Former Commissioner of the Royal Canadian Mounted Police and
Past President of Interpol (retains position of Honorary President to Interpol)

PREFACE

I am honored to write this preface for Perry William Kelly's book, *The Thinking Officer's Guide to Police Defensive Tactics.*

Mr. Kelly has been a student of mine in the Filipino Martial Arts of Kali, Eskrima, Kuntao, Silat and Jun Fan Gung Fu (Bruce Lee's Jeet Kune Do) for several years. His skills and knowledge have enabled him to obtain the rank of instructor in these arts.

His insight and technical ability is proven by this book, which contains information vital to the survival skills of law enforcement personnel. The ability to understand the mentality and techniques utilized by today's criminal element, along with the understanding and application of such techniques, are of the utmost importance to today's law enforcement agencies.

Much can be learned from this comprehensive and highly informative book.

DAN INOSANTO

Mr. Inosanto is a highly-respected martial artist, author and film star. In addition to movie roles with such major action stars as Bruce Lee, Burt Reynolds, Kurt Russell and Steven Segal, Mr. Inosanto was also featured in the police training film Surviving Edged Weapons. *He was chosen by the late Bruce Lee to continue the development of Jeet Kune Do and has previously been honored by* Black Belt *magazine as "Instructor of the Year."*

As the Former Solicitor General of Canada, one of my concerns was the safety of the men and women who police this country. Too often, these individuals are injured or killed while trying to serve and protect those who rely on them.

One of my Departmental officials, Mr. Perry William Kelly, shares this concern. For the past two decades, Mr. Kelly has attempted to enhance the survival skill and defensive tactics of police officers through his articles in several police magazines and through his teachings.

While recognizing his past contributions to police officer safety, I am happy to see that Mr. Kelly has put together a text of this material which will be an asset to the law enforcement community.

THE HONORABLE HERB GRAY, M.P.
Deputy Prime Minister of Canada, Former Solicitor General of Canada

ACKNOWLEDGMENTS

I would like to acknowledge the following people: my wife Valerie for her contributions to this book and my life; my parents for their faith, support and love; the staff of the Library of the Solicitor General of Canada (Heather, Noella, Leonard, France) for their assistance over the many years that this book has been in preparation; my training partners Guro/Kru Robert Carver and Staff Sgt. Graham Muir for their review of the contents of this book; Mr. Jim Kendrick, former intelligence officer and fighter, for his proofreading skills; Ms. Julie MacKinnon, editor of the *RCMP Gazette*, for graciously accepting my work over the years; Mr. Chris D'Amico for his computer wizardry; Joanne Ritchie for her enthusiastic editing skills; and all my instructors, students, sparring partners, and opponents who have all contributed to any knowledge that I may possess.

INTRODUCTION

Let me begin by clarifying that I am not a police officer. I am a lawyer who is employed as a senior policy advisor in the police and law enforcement directorate of the Solicitor General of Canada. However, my life experience, education, training, and work have provided me with considerable insight into police and correctional officer safety.

Looking back, I often wonder how a working-class kid like me, the first person in my family to go to university, never became mixed up in the "criminal life," as I grew up with a number of individuals who ended up on the wrong side of prison bars. One of my childhood friends, the son of a police detective, became an armed robber. I learned of this development, having lost touch with him some years earlier, when his fingerprints were shown on a pistol as part of a demonstration in my forensic science course in law school. In addition, two of my friends from high school were killed in drug deals that went sour. And, one of my teenage kickboxing sparring partners ended up being a hit man who was convicted for killing an ex-narcotics officer.

Luckily, I had strong family ties that prevented me from taking the wrong road. I had cousins and an uncle who were police officers, two in Canada's capital and one with the Royal Canadian Mounted Police (RCMP); I have another cousin who is a court escort officer. My two best friends from university work in the field of corrections. My uncle, who is the survivor of a lethal force encounter, used to baby-sit me by locking me in a cell and letting me play inmate while he picked up his paycheck. Perhaps spending those times in jail made a greater impact than I imagined.

As I said earlier, my work has also contributed to my "education" about police and criminals. After I was called to the bar of the province of Ontario, I spent four years working as an investigator for the Office of the Correctional Investigator. I fondly remember this period as my post-graduate training in prison weapons, smuggling, extortion and violence. I travelled across Canada visiting all the federal prisons, interviewing serial killers, murderers and other types of criminals. I then worked for the Correctional Service of Canada before becoming the first investigator hired by the newly-created RCMP Public Complaints Commission. I eventually became the Assistant Director of Operations and, because of my martial arts background, became the Commission's in-house use of force expert. In this latter capacity, I was called upon to conduct research and to prepare the commission's legal counsel for two public hearings that the commission held on the RCMP's use of the carotid neck restraint.

As far as martial arts go, I have been practicing since I was a child. My father studied Karate in the 1950s and Ju-Jitsu in the 1960s and taught me for a couple of years before sending me for formal training in Karate at age 8 or 9. As a child, I was fortunate to be able to meet and train briefly with Dr. Tsuyoshi Chitose (founder of Chito-Ryu Karate). Coming out of university, I had been a black belt and kickboxer for a number of years. I helped put myself through law school teaching self-defense to other students, personnel of a psychiatric hospital and inner-city kids. Over the last 30 years, I have been certified as an instructor in Ju-Jitsu, Thai boxing, Jun Fan Gung Fu/Jeet Kune Do, Filipino Martial Arts, and in police defense tactics by Pressure Point Control Tactics (PPCT) Management Systems. I have also studied Western boxing, Wing Chun Gung Fu, Savate, Kendo (Japanese fencing), Krabi-Krabong (Thai weaponry), shootfighting and Maphilindo Silat.

My interest in police defensive tactics came initially as a result of Ju-Jitsu and kickboxing training under Prof. Georges Sylvain, a former military and civilian police officer and head of Defence Tactics in the Law and Security faculty at Algonquin College in Ottawa, Canada. Prof. Sylvain created Can-Ryu Ju-Jitsu (his system of Ju-Jitsu which comprises elements designed specifically for police and prison officers) and invented the Algonquin College Sure Grip "Scepter" police baton. As part of my training under him I had to learn and teach searching techniques, restraints, prisoner escort techniques and how to use the police baton.

While studying Ju-Jitsu, I began training with Sgt. Robert Proulx and Sgt. Bernie Ladouceur, defensive tactics instructors for the

Ottawa-Carleton Regional Police. Sgt. Proulx, now retired and a consultant/trainer to many police services, is an expert witness on police defensive tactics, a former defensive tactics instructor at the Ontario Police College, and the survivor of a gunfight which left him with four bullet wounds.

I was also very fortunate to train with Mr. Robert Carver since 1988. In addition to being president of the Thai Boxing Association of Canada and a certified instructor in a number of martial arts including Filipino Martial Arts, Jun Fan Gung Fu, and Maphilindo Silat under Guro Dan Inosanto and Thai boxing under Ajarn Chai Sirisute, he is also a PPCT Management Systems instructor-trainer. Mr. Carver was also the instructor to the RCMP's Special Emergency Response Teams for a number of years. Through my association with him, I have been provided the opportunity to work with police and military tactical response personnel from both Canada and the United States.

Having worked both sides of the bars I am in a unique position. I have spent 15 years studying and discussing with inmates and street criminals what techniques they want to use on police and prison personnel, and I have spent twice that long learning and teaching what techniques the latter use to defend themselves.

For the past 10 years, I have been writing articles for the RCMP Gazette concerning police defensive tactics. After having combed through countless texts on police self-defense training as part of the research process for these articles, I decided to use the fruits of my investigation to write this book. My research has led me to believe that the majority of police defensive tactics books, as one would expect, focus on the teaching of specific techniques. They are usually replete with step by-step illustrations on how to perform certain techniques. Some of them provide a smattering of background information preceding the pictures, but this is there usually just there to set up the visual rendering.

While access to such books is one way of learning defensive tactics, I have always felt that learning through texts has many drawbacks. More often than not, people buy a book and, when they cannot master the techniques shown, become frustrated and discard it. Why is this the case? Quite simply, texts do not provide the elements, other than visual perception of a technique, required to master the technique. To adequately master any technique you must view it, experience its application on you, and apply it on someone else—in slow motion to learn the technique and during sparring to see if you can make it work. As well, most texts do not cover how to overcome problems or enhance the application of techniques.

I am a firm believer in training with a qualified instructor on a regular basis. I know that some of you are thinking that this is not always feasible, especially if you are stationed at a site which does not have access to instructors. Travelling to seminars given by qualified people is one way of overcoming the limitations of learning from a book or video. In my own case, I had been studying books and instructional videotapes produced by my instructors, Guro Dan Inosanto and Ajarn Chai Sirisute, for some years. However, I found that I was able to make more rapid advances in learning from them by experiencing "hands on" seminars.

Why, then, would I write a book if I don't believe in people learning techniques from books? While one may have varying degrees of success learning specific techniques from books, much can still be learned. For example, one of the goals of this text is to share with readers the results of my years of research into police defense tactics. Hopefully, your reading of this text will save you time in searching out what skills you need to have, what type of training to seek, and where to find that training. As well, I believe that the intellectual side of the martial arts (i.e., strategy, theory, technique enhancement, how to critically evaluate a technique, and the like) can be shared in written or verbal form. Too often in our zeal to accomplish a new physical skill, we fail to listen to the verbal instructions given with the physical demonstration or think about how the technique would be applied in actual combat. A case in point is when I teach knife defense. When I teach this type of course, I always preface the empty-hand training by saying that these are techniques of last resort, when escape or other options (e.g., cover, armed response) are not possible. Routinely, whenever I conduct a refresher course, most students have retained only the empty-hand techniques.

If you limit your search for defensive tactics information to the acquisition of physical skills, you are missing a great deal. If you think tactically and translate your thoughts into actions, this can go far in not having to rely on physical force. Every technique starts with an idea. The more ways your brain can imagine a technique going wrong, and how you would refine that technique through critical evaluation as a precursor to physical testing of that technique in the gym, the better chance you have of making that technique work in the street.

A further goal of this book is to make you think about a number of things. The sections covering what the bad guys out there know should make you think about what can happen to you. It should also make you think about obtaining additional training in areas where you are lacking. The sections covering various elements of defensive tactics training should make you think about your current self-defense techniques, why they are not working for you, and how you can enhance them.

In my opinion, the mind is the key to any human interaction which may escalate to the point where defensive tactics are necessary. Clear thinking, a survival mentality, and well thought out strategies and tactics may (and I do stress *may*) allow an officer to anticipate, avoid, or expeditiously conclude a physical confrontation in an appropriate fashion.

Keeping an open mind to new approaches is also a key to successful defensive tactics. Going into a situation thinking you have all the answers, or setting up a training program which is stagnant, can be disastrous. Any law enforcement officer, administrator, or agency head will reap significant benefits by opening themselves to new approaches. I hope that after reading this book, you have also opened up your mind to other ways of looking at the subject of police defensive tactics, some of which I have presented. I would encourage all law enforcement officers, trainers, administrators and policymakers to use the information contained in this book to assist in the analysis and development of their existing police defensive tactics and training regimes.

Finally, it is my hope that this book makes you think more tactically as you do your job. The more you think before you act, the less you will have to react, and the greater chance you stand of getting home without getting hurt or having to hurt someone else.

CONTENTS

THE THINKING OFFICER'S GUIDE
TO POLICE DEFENSIVE TACTICS

Chapter 1

MARTIAL ARTS AND THE POLICE

Over the past 30 years that I have been involved in the martial arts and police training, I have had the opportunity to be exposed to a great many different martial arts, various styles of those arts, and the principles, concepts and techniques found in them. I have discussed martial arts theories with world and Olympic champions, I have trained with world-renowned martial arts masters, and I have ventured to the Orient to enhance my understanding of combat. I have trained barroom bouncers and amateur and professional fighters, and taught civilian, military and correctional special response team personnel.

The purpose of relaying this information is not to blow my own horn that I am the last word in martial arts or police training. I am the first one to admit that my time in these areas has simply opened my eyes to how much more I have to learn about the fighting arts. Luckily, I have always kept an open mind to learning, which has enabled me to stay an avid student and researcher of the martial arts and police training.

Part of this research function, when teaching or training law enforcement officers, is that I have probed their minds for their views with regard to martial arts, as well as the kinds of defensive tactics systems, concepts, principles or techniques they felt would be helpful for their work. I have also tried to discover why certain systems, concepts, principles or techniques are unsuitable for law enforcement.

What I offer for the reader's consideration are my insights into this research. I will begin by discussing what police think about martial arts and artists and why such thinking may be dangerous. I will also try to acquaint police officers with some emerging trends in the combative

3

arts in the new millennium. The basic elements of some of the more universal emerging trends will be covered, and should readers wish more information, they can refer to the source material contained in the Bibliography.

I will then examine a number of different martial arts principles, training and fighting concepts or techniques which my research has led me to believe would be helpful to law enforcement officers in their work and which I would suggest that they explore.

A POLICE VIEW OF MARTIAL ARTS AND ARTISTS

While the majority of martial artists are law-abiding citizens, there are those who make use of what they have learned for nefarious purposes. The media attention achieved by these individuals has often acted as a deterrent to those trying to change the sometimes negative public image regarding martial arts.

Police and prison personnel should be aware of various emerging trends in the martial arts. Too often, an officer's perception of the martial arts may have been shaped by what has appeared on television and in films, or due to a single encounter with a practitioner. This can often lead to perceptions which do not reflect the current state of the arts. A present trend in the martial arts is the focus on practicality. Those involved in the arts have found, as have many officers, that what works in the gym, dojo or dojang, does not necessarily work on the street. Upon discovering that they are not the "black belt experts" they thought they were, some martial artists have sought out specialized skills to bolster their fighting prowess.

Emerging Trends

To supplement their kicking ability and remedy their difficulty in applying powerful hand techniques, martial arts students have taken a page from the boxing textbook. The ability to box has become the skill to be mastered by any practitioner who wants to become involved in full-contact sparring.

To reduce their chances of being defeated by an opponent who is physically stronger or skilled in grappling, modern martial artists have incorporated wrestling or grappling techniques and progressive strength training into their practice schedules. The goal of creating a well-rounded fighter, who can attack or defend with power at any range, is currently in vogue at many schools. If one is practicing for self-defense purposes, logic would dictate that this should be the goal.

As a result of this new trend, the police officer is faced with a more versatile adversary. The officer can no longer discount the "Karate expert" as being ineffective once physically restrained. The modern, pragmatic combatant will have discarded techniques which do not possess devastation potential, or techniques not ruthlessly practical for street confrontations.

During the 1970s in Canada, several martial arts weapons were classified as prohibited. The historical origins of these weapons is less glamorous than one is led to believe. When conquered by Japan, Okinawan peasants began using farm implements as weapons. The *nunchaku* was originally used to beat rice, and the PR-24 or sidehandle nightstick was adapted from a mill tool called a tonfa, or tuifa. The modern martial artist has now focused on weapons which are legal to carry today, and in deference to their ancestors, they have also done some innovating of their own.

The walking stick is presently enjoying a renewed popularity not seen since the days of the dandies in the 1890s, and the pocketknife is considered fashionable for those "dressing for success" in the urban jungle. There will probably be an instructional article on one or both of these weapons in almost any martial arts magazine you pick up these days.

The emergence of the Filipino Martial Arts (FMA) of Kali, Arnis de Mano, and Eskrima, which teach the use of weapons before empty-hand techniques, has often been accused of creating the popularity of weapons training. The Filipino "balisong" or butterfly knife was banned from importation by the U.S. Customs' Service in July 1986. This knife was touted as the "*nunchaku* of the eighties."

As innovative police training personnel placed the PR-24 into police officers' hands, FMA techniques seem now to be gaining acceptance. Unfortunately, Filipino stick and knife techniques may also be finding their way into the repertoire of the criminal element. The application of outdated subject-disarming tactics may well lead to officer injury or death when confronting a suspect trained in these skills. (Further information on the FMA is found in Chapter 7.)

The martial artist's historical ability to be innovative was touched on earlier. Today's practitioners also have that ability, as evidenced by an 1980 article by Joe Zeloof, entitled "Using Tools as Weapons," where the author covers the use of modern-day house tools as weapons. One can only imagine a long-dead Okinawan peasant looking down and admiring the resourcefulness of today's practitioners.

While flipping through the pages of any martial arts magazine published in the 1980s, the craze of Ninja-mania should become apparent to even a casual observer. Historically, the Ninja were hired assassins and spies in feudal Japan. Though a recognized martial art, it contains many elements which intrigue the criminal mind: the ability to master stealth, entry, escape and evasion, weapons concealment, combat and assassination techniques. One notorious Canadian prison escapee who, when arrested, had a handcuff key taped inside his navel, may well be on his way to becoming a homegrown Ninja.

MARTIAL ARTS PRINCIPLES THAT OFFICERS SHOULD EXPLORE

The information detailed below is divided into principles, training and fighting concepts, and techniques. Principles can be defined as overall strategies in relation to fighting. Training and fighting concepts are ways in which one's abilities can be honed. Techniques are those things that one does in an altercation to arrive at one's goal of subduing the opponent.

I have derived the information contained in this part from various martial arts that I have studied. This is not to suggest that other martial arts or defensive tactics systems are not worthwhile; most systems of combat contain elements that could be useful for police. The reason why I have chosen these is detailed in part below and is also discussed in further chapters. What I have offered is only some of the knowledge that can be gained by exploring these systems. I hope that it tempts you to look into them further.

Principles

Finding Your Own Path

One of the first principles that you as an officer should explore is to search for your own personal path, that is, to develop a personal style of fighting that is suited to your particular build and temperament. While further information on this principle is set out in Chapter 9 on defensive tactics and the smaller officer, suffice it to say, if you are of smaller stature and easygoing temperament, you should not be training to fight like Mike Tyson. This principle comes from Jeet Kune Do (JKD) which is more than a martial art, encompassing a collection of concepts about self-defense developed by the late Bruce Lee that can be used to enhance any style of martial art.

Attribute Development

A further principle of JKD worth examining is development of one's attributes. Attributes can be defined as those things that enhance an individual's character and performance. JKD instructor, writer, and movie fight choreographer Burton Richardson, with whom I was lucky enough to train some years ago, lists them as follows (to his list I offer, in parenthesis, my understanding of these elements):

- Health and fitness;
- Attitude (the ability to be in control or bring out the "killer instinct" when necessary, e.g., during a lethal force encounter);
- Timing (the ability to execute a move at the precise moment in time);
- Precision or accuracy in execution of techniques (the ability to successfully complete your technique);
- Speed (the ability to hit, advance on your opponent, or evade quickly);
- Power and strength (the ability to use muscular strength and striking power) ;
- Coordination (the ability to execute moves in sequence);
- Sensitivity (visual–the ability to "read" an opponent, or tactile–the ability to "feel" the next move of an opponent by body pressure);
- Rhythm (the ability to follow a beat and move in broken rhythm fashion);
- Knowledge (e.g., knowing that a kick in the groin can be a disabling technique);
- Experience (e.g., knowing that the groin kick can be used against you when you exit a suspect, feet first, from the rear of your unit.
- Durability (the ability to absorb punishment without giving up during a confrontation);

- Balance (the ability move and execute techniques without stumbling or falling to the ground);
- Relaxation (the ability not to become too tight and unfluid in an altercation);
- Endurance (the ability to keep from running out of gas during a confrontation);
- Mobility and agility (the ability to use distance and balance to your advantage);
- Flexibility (the ability to stretch the muscles and tendons); and
- Flow (the ability to move from one technique to another–this attribute is more fully examined in Chapter 7 on FMA and its applicability to law enforcement baton training).

Keeping an Open Mind

One of the key principles of JKD is keeping an open mind. Unlike some other martial arts, JKD practitioners do not see their way as the only way. Cross-training in different martial arts, different styles, and with different instructors is encouraged as a knowledge-expanding experience.

Ranges of Combat

A JKD principle that is often overlooked by other martial arts is that there are different ranges of combat. For example, you may be the hardest puncher since Joe Louis, but that may not help you if you are attacked when in a telephone booth. JKD practitioners train to be effective at all ranges of combat. One of those ranges that can be found in JKD is trapping. Trapping can also be defined as holding or checking your opponent's limbs while you deliver a strike. The beauty of trapping is that very few people know how to fight in this range, and it allows one to enter from long range to close range without getting injured. The ranges of combat are explained more fully in Chapter 5 on joint locking.

Hard Core Fighting Mentality

One of the principles in Thai boxing which should be explored by the police is its approach to fighting. Thai boxing adopts a hard-core mentality for fighting that teaches fighters to keep on going despite injury. While in Thailand, I witnessed one boxer get kneed so hard in the stomach that he lost his dinner. Despite being hit that hard, he picked himself off the mat and went on to win the fight. My companion at the fight, a former member of a national championship amateur football team, called it the "gutsiest performance" he had ever seen in sports.

While I would not advocate that police officers trade blows during a confrontation to show how much punishment they can take, adopting a survival attitude of not accepting pain or entertaining the thought of giving up is a training principle that deserves exploration, because on the street surrender can be fatal.

Always Expect a Weapon

One principle which has the greatest overlap with police defensive tactics comes from the FMA. When one is involved in any physical altercation, always expect a weapon to come into play. Filipino martial artists learn the weapon before the empty hand and often train both together to ensure that this principle is not forgotten.

Learn to Use the Weapon to be Able to Defend Against It

Above, I alluded to an FMA principle which deserves exploration, that is, to teach the use of the weapon before the empty hand. In addition to teaching one to expect a weapon, this is done so that one can appreciate the strengths and limitations of any weapon. Knowing how to use a weapon broadens your understanding of how to defend against it.

Tactical Advantage

Another principle of FMA that is key to police defensive tactics is that of tactical advantage. By tactical advantage I mean that an opponent may have one or many weapons when they confront you, and these may be exposed or secreted for use as back-ups. In the same way that a police officer feels comfort in the fact that multiple weapons are better than one, by having a baton, pepper spray, and, a hideout ankle gun to enhance his or her sidearm, so may their adversary.

You may have already heard others ascribe to this principle during your career without knowing it. It is commonly stated by the following police pearl of wisdom: Never bring a knife to a gunfight.

Similar Responses to Similar Angles of Attack

In the FMA, similar techniques can be used to defend against a baton strike, knife slash or stab, or an empty-hand strike if they all follow the same angle of attack. As well, these defenses can be done with either the empty hand or with the baton. The ability to apply similar defensive tactics to any type of attack along a certain angle simplifies one's reactions. In physical confrontations, simple techniques that employ gross motor skills are always easier to implement.

Analyze and Exploit an Opponent's Weaknesses

The one principle that I would recommend that police officers explore from the grappling arts of Judo, Aikido, wrestling, and the like, is that of analyzing and exploiting an opponent's weakness. For example, from judo and aikido, we learn that one should not oppose force but rather go with it to unbalance an opponent, thereby exploiting that weakness. From the other grappling and locking arts, we analyze the human body and exploit its weak points by applying pressure to joints and tendons. By learning to analyze and exploit the weaknesses of others, we also learn our own. Such a journey of self discovery need not be limited to the realm of defensive tactics, it can also applied to other facets of our life.

Attack an Opponent's Balance

A further principle related to exploiting an opponent's weaknesses which can be found in Silat, a catchall term for various grappling and striking arts found in Indonesia, Malaysia, and the Philippines, is to exploit the weaknesses in a person's balance. Watching a fight involving someone who is skilled in Silat leaves one incredulous. All of a sudden, the attacker just drops to the ground in a most unforgiving manner. Why is this important for police officers? Think of how easy the officer's job would be if anyone who became violent with them suddenly lost their balance. It is pretty difficult for most people to inflict injury when they are lying on their back or their face.

Nice Guys and Gals Finish Last

To street fighters, there is no such thing as the Marquis of Queensbury rules, they will do anything to win. This is a good principle to remember when engaged in a serious confrontation with a street fighter. Closely linked to that principle is the use of weapons by street fighters. They will use hidden, disguised and improvised weapons if they get a chance; so should any officer if the situation demands it. More information on hidden, disguised, and improvised weapons is provided in Chapter 3.

I have included street fighting in this section because in my mind this is a martial art. While it may not have a belt ranking system, honor, or etiquette, it does have instructors and students who exchange techniques and practice them—on people in your line of work!

Training and Fighting Concepts

Stop-Hitting

Bruce Lee adapted this JKD concept from the sport of fencing. A stop-hit is accomplished by striking an opponent as he or she attacks you, and eliminating the need for blocking. A simple example is to deliver a stiff jab as your opponent winds up to hit you with a haymaker.

Thai Pad Training

Thai boxing (or Muay Thai) is the national sport of Thailand and resembles North American kickboxing with a few exceptions. These are that fighters, in addition to their hands and feet, can strike with their knees and elbows. They can also deliver devastating kicks to the legs. No other martial art has been able to consistently beat Thai boxing at its own game.

One of the training concepts boxers employ is the use of Thai pads (forearm pads that a student can hit while the trainer stalks, evades, or retaliates). This is a training concept that should be looked into by anyone involved in self-defense. Too often, we test out our striking power on inanimate objects that remain stationary or don't hit back. The most common example is training on the heavy punching bag. Thai pad training, where you hit a target and it can hit you back, makes your training more closely resemble an actual physical confrontation. A further discussion on this type of realistic training is found in Appendix A on training aids.

Realistic Sparring

Full-contact sparring is used in both boxing and Thai boxing. Actually hitting someone and having them hit you if you do not evade or block is far different from going through the motions. During this kind of training, you will not get lulled into thinking a technique will work unless it does work on you or on that non-compliant individual you are mixing it up with.

A grappling variation of the above-mentioned striking example is use of *randori* (free sparring) in judo where both parties are seeking to end the session with a submission lock or a strangulation. This type of training makes the training mat a chemistry set where constant experimentation takes place to see what really works in combat and what only works in theory. Such training will also demonstrate why the attributes mentioned earlier must be trained on a regular basis. Rolling around on the mats will quickly make a believer out of anyone who thinks they can survive a street confrontation without a proper level of conditioning and skills training.

Sharpening the Reflexes Through Weapons Training

Because a stick or knife can be maneuvered at speeds faster than the hand, any defensive skills training against these weapons will make one's defenses to empty-hand attacks much quicker. This type of FMA training is also more beneficial to police officers trying to increase their reflexes than other types of exercise, because the individual is learning a new set of survival skills while training this attribute.

Fighting from Unorthodox Positions

One of Silat's training concepts that is valuable and should be explored is that students learn to apply their techniques from the sitting, lying and squatting postures. Anyone who has seen any number of street confrontations will tell you that they are not stand-up slugfests seen in the movies but most often result in one or both parties going to the ground. This is especially true on slippery, icy, muddy or sandy terrain. If you, as a police officer, happen to be the one that hits the ground first, it would be a major asset to know how to defend yourself from that position.

Train Under the Same Conditions as You Would Have to Fight

Street fighters train under the same conditions they fight in. They do not wear a *gi* or loose fitting sweat clothes because they will not be fighting in them—they wear their regular clothes. Savate, the art of French foot fighting, is based on street-fighting. Consequently, they wear shoes when they train, and the use of the shoe as a street fighting weapon has been adapted into the techniques of this martial art.

One street-fighting school I am aware of in Chicago even had a bar set up in it so its students could practice under more lifelike conditions and in the state of intoxication some students would be in when the fight started.

For the police officer, this translates into dressing in an old uniform, including that heavy winter parka, boots, and all your police equipment, and practicing your defensive tactics skills. One will quickly learn how this impairs mobility, speed, and endurance. As well, one learns what pieces of one's uniform can be a liability (e.g., that microphone cord becomes an inviting improvised garrote while rolling around on the ground).

Techniques

Finger Jab

Any person familiar with JKD or Jun Fan Gung Fu (the style of Gung Fu developed by Bruce Lee) will probably employ a technique known as the "finger jab." In this technique, the extended fingers are jabbed at the eyes. The beauty of this technique for police usage is that contact does not have to be made with the eyes. It is also a great technique to distract someone, allowing you to use a more appropriate follow-up technique. However, should it be a life-or-death struggle, this is a very fast and potentially crippling technique.

Thai Round Kick

One Thai boxing technique that has already found its way into police defensive tactics is the Thai round kick. PPCT Management Systems has a leg strike to the common peroneal and lateral femoral nerves of the leg which closely parallels the Thai round kick. Learning how to deliver the PPCT version like a Thai round kick would enable officers to use this commonly accepted police strike with more power and mobility.

Knee and Elbow Strikes

No other martial art I have seen uses the knees and elbows like Thai boxing. While it is true that other martial arts have the same strikes and can generate unbelievable amounts of power with them, no other martial art can deliver these strikes as quickly or with footwork as mobile as Thai boxing. They are used by the Thais at relatively close range and are devastating personal defense tools which can make the difference for police officers whose safety is in danger and must rely on their empty-hand skills to quickly incapacitate an attacker.

Nerve Strikes

The FMA have many nerve strikes which can be of particular use to the police officer. These arts teach how to knee the thighs, elbow the bicep, kick the shins, and stomp the ankles from a position that is surprisingly similar to the police "escort position" (where the hands are holding the elbow of the individual). These simple stunning techniques from the escort position can be invaluable to overcome a reluctant arrestee with minimal effort and without causing injury to the individual.

Joint Locking

From Ju-Jitsu, Judo, Dumog, Aikido, shootfighting, and wrestling, I would suggest that officers explore joint locks that can be learned easily and applied simply. While most arts have numerous locks, I would suggest that officers learn, master, and maintain a few that they can apply in most situations with an unwilling participant.

From shootfighting and Filipino Dumog, I would also encourage officers to learn "lock flows." Lock flows are a training technique whereby locks can be practiced in a pre arranged manner. The "flow" or sequence of locks that one practices is based on how a person would attempt to escape from the preceding lock. For example, if one is applying a wrist lock and the individual straightens his or her arm to escape the pain, the flow would dictate that you should lock the elbow that is now vulnerable.

When I am engaging in grappling practice, I also try to blend together the techniques of the different grappling and joint-locking arts that I have studied. I try to flow from one art to another as the opportunity permits. This is a JKD concept that should be explored. No one art has all the answers, nor should it.

The Dumog Shoulder Wrench and Silat Sweep

Filipino Dumog (the grappling and locking portion of the FMA) also offers a technique which fits into the fighting concept of attacking a person's balance called a shoulder wrench. From the escort position, this technique can be used to destabilize the subject, if he should try to strike you while being escorted.

One Silat technique which also relates to attacking balance and is highly applicable to police officers is a takedown from the escort position. Silat practitioners, when they encounter resistance from the escort position, merely kick back and sweep out one of the individual's legs, causing him or her to drop to the ground on the stomach. It has the advantages of being quite easy to learn, requiring very little effort to accomplish, and results in placing an individual in a position where handcuffs can easily be applied. More specific information concerning these arts is provided in Chapter 5 on joint locks, come-alongs and pain compliance holds.

Street-Fighting Techniques

Street-fighting techniques that police officers should be aware of run the gamut from head butts to ripping, clawing and gouging, biting, pinching, and spitting. While other martial arts also contain many of the same techniques, they are usually reserved for a situation where more traditional techniques fail.

CONCLUSION

The intention of this chapter is to free you from any preconceived notions you may have had about martial arts and their practitioners. It is also intended to expose you to various fighting systems you may have not been aware of previously. Hopefully, such exposure will have wetted a few appetites to explore these arts. In much the same way as one would learn about various types of police equipment that might be useful at work, I would encourage officers to take the time to look into any of the arts.

Chapter 2

PRISONS AS GLADIATOR SCHOOLS

Some years back, I reviewed a video on police officer weapon retention produced by the Los Angeles County Sheriff's Department. It made reference to the idea that inmates in the U.S. were learning lessons in prison on how to disarm police officers of their firearms. The 1970s TV movie *Jericho Mile* coined perhaps the most appropriate term for this phenomenon of inmates acquiring lessons in violence, when one of the characters called prisons "gladiator schools."

During the five years I worked as an investigator and analyst in the Canadian prison system, and in the years since then, I have attempted to examine the validity of the concept that the prison experience is schooling inmates in tactics of violence. From my perspective as a defensive tactics instructor who has taught patrol officers and institutional emergency response officers, I propose to share some information I have gathered which demonstrates that this concept might be true.

Why is this topic important to police and prison personnel? I am sure some readers are saying, "I don't care what they do or learn in prison." Having spent thousands of hours interviewing inmates and countless more researching defensive tactics, I can safely say that law enforcement officers should care about what inmates might be learning in prison. From an officer survival perspective, it makes sense to be aware of the myriad of things inmates can learn or activities they can participate in while in custody, which can pose a danger to you.

Some critics might be saying, "Once they're off the street I can forget about them." This type of reasoning is tenuous for three reasons. First, you should know that the information I obtained from inmate sources most pertinent to this topic did not come from my interviews with alleged or convicted serial killers like Clifford Olson, Charles Ng, and Allen Legere, "the beast of the Miramichi," who are probably incarcerated for life, or were deported from Canada to the U.S., as in the case of Ng. The information came from inmates serving specific periods of incarceration for a number of different offenses and who will eventually be released. Therefore, as patrol officers you may run into them again. Should your paths cross upon their release, you should know what tactics they may have learned which can be used against you prior to experiencing them in a potentially fatal encounter. Second, for those readers who are custodial personnel, the information inmates acquire can pose a danger to you during their incarceration. Finally, these personnel should be aware of this negative learning/education (generic terms I will use to cover acquiring knowledge of criminal tactics and techniques) that inmates may be exposed to, in order to prevent the acquisition of this information from continuing unchecked.

In addition to the input from inmate sources mentioned above, other sources of information used in the preparation of this chapter include extensive discussions with prison officials in both the U.S. and Canada, investigators and defensive tactics instructors, and a thorough examination of prison incident reports, media articles and books written by inmates on prison subculture.

I do not mean to suggest that institutional security personnel or other prison authorities are lax in their vigilance in curtailing inmate involvement in such negative learning. It is trite to say that staff cannot supervise inmates continually and that no rehabilitative strategies employed by staff can totally eliminate all the negative activities carried out by individuals of criminal background while incarcerated. Rehabilitative, educational, or work activities do not occupy the whole of an inmate's day. Inmates have unstructured leisure time which can give rise to the exchange of different criminal tactics.

Having worked in the prison system myself, I realized early that prisons are places where violent people are sent, who, while incarcerated, may commit other violent acts, or have such acts perpetrated against them. Unfortunately, sometimes there is little staff can do to prevent this. It is this environment which provides inmates with opportunities to learn how to do violent things when released.

This chapter will not focus on other types of negative education inmates may acquire while incarcerated. Many articles and texts are available which deal with such subjects as strategies employed by criminals to defeat police detection of their crimes, or their conviction in court, as well as strategies employed by criminals to deceive or compromise police investigators, judges and/or juries, parole boards, case management and institutional security personnel, employees of ombuds offices or volunteers. Readers interested in this topic should refer to *Games Criminals Play* (Allen & Bosta, 1981). Information is also available on the ways criminals acquire knowledge on how to successfully commit other types of crimes, e.g., fraud, burglary, or robbery, from their peers.

LEARNING THEORY IN PRISON

We know from psychology that learning best takes place at a younger age when we are most impressionable. We also know from crime and incarceration statistics that crime is primarily an activity for young adults who do not fully appreciate the end result of their activities or the likelihood of their being apprehended. This is reflected by incarceration statistics which demonstrate that prisons disproportionately contain young people. Because of these factors, inmates are at risk of being socialized in a negative manner.

What kind of learning are we talking about? While this can be an individual actively seeking out such information, this is not necessarily always the case. Much of this learning can be acquired by listening to other more sophisticated inmates. Through interaction with others, the neophyte learns the activities, tactics, and mind-set to make him or her a gladiator.

Often, the lessons of the prison gladiator are also learned by passive observation of incidents of violence between inmates or between inmates and staff. From such observations, the inmate learns which techniques (with or without weapons) will or won't incapacitate or cause injury. As well, they learn what injuries are most likely and how to survive and continue fighting when injured in a certain way.

With this as our premise, let's examine the curriculum an inmate can be exposed to while incarcerated in most prison gladiator schools.

Curriculum

Physical Education

STRENGTH TRAINING. In most institutions I have visited, weight lifting is a key activity. New inmates quickly learn that the one who packs on 20 to 30 pounds of muscle in the iron pit, and can bench press a truck engine, is not going to be harassed by others, irrespective of his or her prowess at fighting. The image projected is one of strength and an ability to defend oneself. Because this image is desired, the activities that give rise to this physique are adopted.

Every few years the debate over whether inmates should be allowed to lift weights surfaces. Proponents of inmate access to weights (most notably inmates themselves) argue that it provides an avenue for inmates to dissipate their frustration and, as such, prevents violence. Opponents of this activity argue that it builds strength which can cause problems by creating inmates who are stronger than the staff who sometimes have to physically subdue them.

When working out in a prison gym, the inmate also learns what types of lifts put someone in a vulnerable position for a surprise attack, i.e., squats and bench press. As well, the inmate learns that weight-lifting equipment itself can be used as improvised weapons. One inmate I knew quite well had a knee dislocated and a leg broken when attacked with a 60-pound bar while he was bench pressing. He continued fighting. Think about that next time you forego a physical training session.

Despite the protestations of inmates, some correctional facilities have attempted to eliminate the weights as weapons by using only weight-lifting machines. One institution I visited even had all the dumbbells soldered so that small plates could not be thrown discus like at staff, as had occurred in the past.

During periods when access to weights is curtailed, such as a lockdown or period spent in segregation, other strength-building exercises such as push-ups and sit-ups done in cells are substituted. It is not uncommon for an inmate to do 1,000 push-ups and sit-ups daily to fight the boredom of such periods.

AEROBICS. While running will never suppress weight lifting as a prime prison activity, some institutions have tracks or some other place to run. This activity bolsters the aerobic capacity which can aid a criminal to escape apprehension when being chased or can provide additional staying power when involved in a violent confrontation with law enforcement or custodial personnel.

MARTIAL ARTS. Like weight lifting, there is a debate about the practice of Asian martial arts in prison. Proponents and detractors voice arguments similar to those detailed earlier regarding inmate access to weight lifting. In most institutions, not only is martial arts sparring banned, but Kata (prearranged fighting forms) are also banned. Tai Chi is usually permitted, because it is felt that performing the 108 movements in its form would have a meditative, calming effect on inmates similar to non-incarcerated practitioners.

What is interesting from a defensive tactics perspective is that often these same institutions allow a Western martial art, boxing, to be practiced regularly. Inmates in most institutions today can regularly punch the heavy bag and shadow box without sanction. Incredibly, some U.S. prisons even permit competitive boxing programs while outlawing other martial arts. The boxing program at Rahway State Prison in New Jersey even produced a top professional boxing contender named James Scott some years back.

As for Tai Chi, anyone who has ever felt the combat applications of the art which are contained in the 108 movements can attest to their effectiveness, yet practicing the movements of this martial art form is permissible in prison.

Lastly, with regard to martial arts while in gladiator school, the pupil will have the opportunity to view the strategies employed in attacks by multiple individuals. He or she will learn how one individual will distract (verbally or visually) or restrain the target while the other individual ambushes the victim. It is highly possible that inmates might use these techniques at a later time against officers or be aware that they may be used by officers trying to restrain them.

Health Studies

During incarceration, gladiators in training discover that access to a number of things which were probably not part of their life-style prior to incarceration, i.e., proper diet, health and dental care, and regimented sleep times, will enhance their strength and combative training.

In contrast to these positive factors, because some of the negative aspects of their life-style on the street can also be found in gladiator schools, i.e., abuse of alcohol, homemade "brew" and drugs, inmates also learn the ability to function, camouflage the effects of, or fight while under the influence of drugs or alcohol.

Applied Arts: Police Sciences

During their stay at gladiator school, inmates may become skilled in some of the same courses you would have taken at your training academy. Subjects such as searching, frisking, handcuffing, evidence collection, fingerprinting, firearm retention, and weapons use are learned in prison, but with a very different focus.

The inmate would first learn the art of "frisk foiling," learning where to conceal weapons in their rooms or vehicle or on their body so they won't be found during a frisk or search. Our neophyte gladiator will also learn how to access these weapons quickly to assault an officer or how to dispose of the evidence after usage.

Tied in with how to avoid being caught with contraband during a search would be methods to incapacitate an officer during a search. The inmate would learn that fishhooks sewn into the seams of pants will trap officers' hands if they slide their hands down the legs of a person being searched. The inmate would also learn how to disable or disarm an officer who relies upon a "prop" search (more information on "prop" searches can be found in Chapter 4). Inmates also learn how to pick handcuff and leg-restraint locks.

Inmates become familiar with bladed weapon fighting because "shanks" are used routinely in prison. Some inmates continue to favor this weapon upon release because a pocketknife is legal and can be easily hidden. During his or her time at gladiator school, the inmate, out of necessity, through observation or use, will gain familiarity and proficiency with bladed weapons. In the video *Surviving Edged Weapons* by Calibre Press, one scene, in fact, shows a group of inmates, photographed by a surveillance camera, practicing knife-fighting techniques for use during searches. Lastly, with regard to shanks, it is not by coincidence that handles of homemade knives in prison are covered with twine or rags. Use of these materials on the handle prevents slippage during a bloody assault and fingerprints showing up on the shank. The prevalence of this type of handle construction in most prisons points to the validity of our premise that this knowledge is being passed between inmates.

At your training academy or through in-service training, you probably would have received training in the use of impact weapons and gas or pepper spray. Prison gladiators receive this training too, but with a slight difference. In prison, they have gas or pepper spray used against them and know its effects. They bring this experience with them to the street, as one police officer I trained in knife defense pointed out, when he told me that during an arrest he made, the suspect tried to use pepper spray on him.

Generally, attacks in prisons with impact weapons ("pipings") are used more by inmates to intimidate than to kill. As the prison adage goes, "a piping is warning, a shanking is for keeps." Inmate gladiators do learn how to effectively use and defend against impact weapons, something to remember the next time you pull out your nightstick.

Before moving on to a different topic, I would briefly like to remind you that almost any article within reach can be used as an improvised weapon. One medium security institution inmate applied this knowledge of spotting and using improvised weapons when he made use of the range toaster to bash another inmate. When I inquired what his motivation was, he replied that he grabbed the first thing he could when the other inmate grasped his testicles and tried to crush them during a fight.

Psychology

During incarceration, our budding gladiators will have a number of antisocial attitudes reenforced by their teachers. They will learn (or have enhanced as some would argue) the following attitudes: the weak are to be preyed upon; compassion and remorse are signs of weakness; the successful criminal is to be admired; and, most importantly, cops and guards are the enemy.

HUMAN NATURE STUDIES: VICTIMOLOGY. Inmates learn very quickly in prison what type of persona to project so they do not become the prey of other inmates. Out of necessity, they become adept at identifying those who won't fight back and those who will. So don't bluff if you are not prepared to "walk the walk" after you've "talked the talk" as they will surely spot this.

In his book *In the Belly of the Beast: Letters from Prison,* inmate Jack Henry Abbott details how inmates learn to lull their victims into being off guard before attacking. Be aware that through words or demeanor, trained fighters will attempt to distract you and bridge the distance between themselves and you prior to an attack.

Political Science

During incarceration, some inmates may become involved with racial supremacist prison gangs or other hate groups whose politically motivated crimes can be categorized as terrorism rather than crimes of passion or crimes for profit. Such groups preach, regardless of their core ideology, that police are the lackeys of the state and should be viewed as potential targets. Therefore, as a police officer you should be on guard during an encounter with a hate criminal even if his or her race is the same as yours. Do not be lulled into thinking that your skin color will keep you from being attacked. To them, police officers are but one color: blue.

Miscellaneous Courses

SHOP. During his or her sojourn as a guest of the state, our budding gladiator learns how to manufacture weapons, and other handy items such as handcuff keys, out of almost anything. The ingenuity of an individual who is in captivity is amazing. Two examples of this are the inmate who fashioned a garotte out of braided toilet paper and another who painstakingly made a metal ball out of layers of cigarette package foil.

Artisans who manufacture weapons in prison, at least the ones I have met, usually steadfastly deny their involvement in such activities and guard their secrets. The Bibliography includes a number of articles and books (Haskew, 1993; Jenks and Brown, 1978; Meany, 1993; Pentecost, 1988) for those who are interested in learning more about how knives are fabricated and used in prison.

ART STUDIES. In addition to decorative tattoos, inmates often bear ones which demonstrate their affiliation with a group that has a propensity for violence, i.e., bikers or skinheads, or are reflective of their time in a certain facility. As well, gang members or other inmates sometimes have tattoos to identify themselves as having committed certain crimes, e.g., a tattoo of teardrops falling from the eyes can sometimes identify a individual who has committed murder. The current popularity of tattoos does not mean an officer should view all tattooed persons as possible threats. However, a visual scan for "alarm bell" tattoos when scanning for weapons can go far to keep you safe.

FASHION STUDIES. Inmates learn that wearing clothes in a certain way can enhance the use of weapons. The oversized leg of trousers can conceal a shotgun slid down it. Leaving a shirt buttoned only at the neck can provide easy access to weapons concealed under it. A bandanna or hairdo can be arranged to conceal a razor blade. Clothes can be layered to "frisk foil." In addition, "double dressing" (wearing a second set of clothes under oversized clothes that can be discarded if bloody or easily identifiable) is learned. Once released, inmates in racist white supremacist gangs may wear red shoelaces in their Doc Martens™ to show that they have spilled blood for their cause. This visual cue can be used by police to quickly identify a potentially violent individual.

In his autobiography *Will*, G. Gordon Liddy, convicted Watergate conspirator, recounts how he was injured during fisticuffs with another inmate who had learned that wearing a "fighting ring" (a ring with sharp raised edges or with the decorative stone removed) while punching can easily cause lacerations.

ELECTRONICS. I once interviewed a maximum-security inmate who was complaining that staff had erroneously labelled him as dangerous. He asked: "How can they say that when they allow me to carry this?" whereupon he took out a metal cylinder from out of his pocket which turned out to be a utility knife for crafts. It was somewhat disconcerting to me that this individual also had the blades for the knife with him and had just been through the metal detector prior to our interview. Exactly how he defeated the weapon-detection system is still a mystery.

CONCLUSION

The notion of prisons as being schools for crime was the plot for a lighthearted television series in the 1980s starring the late Dack

Rambo. The show began with Rambo as the pupil, being told, by one of his prison teachers, one of the most ludicrous lines ever uttered on television: "You never know when precision gymnastics will come in handy!" The real world of prison life is very different. In prison, only the strong survive, and sometimes even the strong don't last. Those who last do so, in my opinion, because they learn how to be gladiators in their arena.

In some prisons, correctional staff are attending lectures being given by gladiators in training. Correctional staff are learning how to fabricate, conceal, carry, and use a "sissy shank" (a toothbrush with a razor blade melted into it), and are thereby learning how to defend against it. If you are dealing with offenders or ex-offenders as part of your work, it is important from a survival perspective for you to be aware of the possible knowledge they may have acquired while incarcerated.

Chapter 3

HIDDEN, DISGUISED, AND IMPROVISED WEAPONS

"Tonight we are going to discuss hidden weapons," the instructor said. The burly city police officer was called on to search the instructor for hidden weapons. A veteran street cop of many years, the officer proceeded through the standard searching method he had been taught years before and had been using since then. When he was finished removing some "nasty" toys, the teacher began to place on the desktop the things the officer had missed. The handcuff key and razor blade taped to the inside of his belt were dismissed as being easily overlooked. The small needles on the back of the lapels of his suit coat were seen as harmless enough, unless the assailant went for the eyes. However, over coffee break that evening everyone remarked about the queasy feeling each of us had when the instructor removed the fiberglass-filled plastic letter opener from the inside of his tie. We all realized what damage this overlooked item was capable of doing. This true-life incident happened at a college course on executive protection I attended early in my career.

It would be beyond the scope of this chapter to discuss the strengths and weaknesses of various methods of conducting suspect or vehicle searches. How they relate to officer weapon retention or the degree of subject control is not the purpose of this chapter. Further discussions with the departmental officer assigned to training would be much more valuable, as nothing can really duplicate the experience garnered from hands on training. Every police officer is, however, encouraged to keep abreast of developments in the area of suspect and vehicle searches. Officers should also remember that all persons they come in contact with are potentially dangerous.

The purpose of this chapter is to bring to the customs, corrections, or police officer's attention information collected by me from a number of sources. This information should increase the officer's vigilance and awareness when effecting a search and perhaps prevent an injury to the officer or others. If by reading this chapter, a single officer prevents an injury by locating a weapon in an area they would have previously dismissed or by removing a suspicious object they would have previously overlooked, then the purpose will have been served.

HIDDEN OR DISGUISED WEAPONS

A newspaper article some years ago showed a picture of a woman removing a derringer from her hair bow. The article was discussing a fashion show in Miami, which was attempting to attract women as firearms customers by showing them they could remain attractive while carrying a concealed weapon. One should take note that while the majority of the text will relate to weapons secreted on male felons, readers should not relax their vigilance when searching a suspect of either sex. However, departmental policy on acceptable behavior when dealing with persons of the opposite sex must always be adhered to.

The wallet gun of the seventies has been replaced by something new, the "beeper" gun, a replica of a portable paging unit which contains a small firearm. The doctor who appears to be raising a beeper to hear a message could be an offender in a stolen lab coat who may be levelling a weapon at you as you approach unsuspectingly.

In addition to wallet guns, a number of other weapons have been confiscated by police agencies worldwide. They include cane guns, ring guns, lighter guns, miniature key chain guns and pen guns, a variation on the stinger or zip gun. The hollowed-out book once used to conceal firearms has been replaced by a book that is manufactured and offered for sale already hollowed out.

Various police publications have alerted their readers to the fact that "outlaw" motorcycle gangs have rigged up shotguns in the handlebars of their motorcycles, and secreted shotguns in the doors of passenger vehicles. In light of the availability of Teflon bullets and exploding ammunition, as was purchased by John Hinkley who attempted to assassinate U.S. President Reagan in 1981, the police officer should not discount a suspicious article by thinking it could not contain a firearm large enough to inflict serious injury.

Bridging the gap between firearms and stabbing/slashing weapons are knife-guns that fire bullets and a device called the "ballistic knife." The latter is a standard-looking knife with a ring attached to the hilt that, once pulled, launches the blade in a projectile fashion toward the adversary. Officers should be wary of any suspect who seems all too willing to hand over his or her knife when requested, especially if it has a ring near the handle.

In North America, the technology of concealment concerning bladed or pick weapons has progressed rapidly since Canada, for example, made the spiked finger ring and belt-buckle knife prohibited weapons in the late seventies. Such weapons can now be found secreted inside parts of canes, riding crops, lipsticks, and in a variety of pens offered for sale in martial arts publications. Some of these concealed blades are hidden in pens which screw together and, in at least one other case, can be projected out, stiletto fashion, by flicking a button.

A one-inch "hideaway" knife is available for sale and should not be discounted due to its small size. A suspect may have passed up on the deterrent aspect of a larger knife because he or she knows how and where to inflict damage with the smaller blade. With various paramilitary magazines showing that a large bladed weapon can be carried undetected in a paper bag, anything the suspect has that could contain a blade should be treated as such until discounted by a thorough search after the suspect is under control and handcuffed.

While firearm and bladed hideout weapons should be of primary concern to the police officer, other non-lethal weapons categories should not be forgotten. Impact and various types of stunning weapons are probably being acquired by possible assailants, as well as lawful citizens purchasing these weapons for their own protection. Various types of stunning weapons have, for many years, been manufactured for citizen and police use in various parts of North America. The stunning methods range from chemical repellent, noise or light blast, to projectile impact and electrical shock.

"Sap" or lead-lined gloves could also be used on the unsuspecting officer. This is more a risk to those officers working in colder climates where sap gloves or "brass knuckle" weapons can be concealed by other gloves or mittens during the winter months. A warm weather variant of the above is a "palm sap" or lead weight hidden under a pair of fingerless biking gloves.

Other types of impact weapons that police officers should be aware of include the telescoping spring-cosh, a cane containing the same, a nightstick that can be converted with a twist of the wrist into a nunchaku, and steel-toed running shoes now available from industrial supply outlets.

The use of the "prowler fouler," a launcher of lead-shot filled bags, figured prominently in the movie *The Hunter*, starring the late Steve McQueen. When triggered, it propelled a bean bag at high speed with a non-lethal but devastating effect. Various electronic stunning weapons are available in some parts of the U.S. but are considered prohibited weapons in Canada. However, Canadian police officers and those of other countries should become acquainted with what is available in the U.S. market to prevent being taken by surprise by an assailant armed with American weapons.

One electronic stunning device delivers a high-voltage stun through electrodes which impale the adversary. At first glance, it could be mistaken for a type of camping or household flashlight. Other types of electric stun weapons come disguised as portable paging units, and some are small enough to be secreted in the palm of the hand. These latter devices require that the user be close enough to touch the adversary when delivering the jolt. Officers can neutralize this weapon by remaining a sufficient distance from the suspect during questioning. This safety zone also prevents being caught off guard by a surprise, unarmed attack.

Disguised weapons which use blasts of sound, light or a chemical agent come in various forms, from key chains to pocket flashlights. What might appear to be a harmless object dangling from a suspect's keys may be what gives the suspect the ability to briefly disorient or incapacitate an officer.

Hopefully, this information will not only increase officers' suspicion of previously disregarded objects but will also enable officers to search without becoming paranoid of every single object. If applied judiciously, successes will warrant the extra time spent conducting a search.

IMPROVISED WEAPONS

When discussing the topic of improvised weaponry, there is a tendency to be distracted by the more sensational aspects which are the stock-in-trade of action adventure writers and movie directors. At its best, knowledge of what can be used as a weapon can prevent the police or correctional officer from allowing someone access to articles which can be used against the officer or others. At its worst, the subject panders to the "Rambo" mentality of those destructive elements of society who use such knowledge in preparation for their imagined confrontations.

Gaining the Upper Hand by Using What's at Hand

The use of everyday articles as weapons has been around since the first cave dweller picked up a rock and bashed someone. Popularized by Trevanian in his novel *Shibumi*, the author states that it was an occult brand of the martial arts known as "Hoda Korosu." Whether such a martial art exists is open to conjecture and is the subject of debate among those interested in the martial arts. What is important, however, for police, customs, and correctional officers to remember, is that ordinary things can be used by persons in custody to inflict injury. The officer should also be aware that specialized instruction is available to the public at large in the form of such books such as *Black Medicine, Volume II: Weapons at Hand* (Mashiro, 1979), which contains a list of over 180 objects that can be used as weapons.

Martial arts magazine writer Timothy Hosey wrote an article in the late 1970s entitled "Street-Smart Fighting: Putting the Environment on Your Side," in which he categorized things the average person could use for self-defense. Hosey's categories, with my elements added in parentheses, are as follows:

- Rangers: weapons that increase the attack range (e.g., sticks, rakes, flexible articles [chains, belts], objects which can be thrown).
- Reinforcers: weapons that increase the striking power or potential for injury (e.g., rocks, bottles held in hand, steel-toed boots, helmets).
- Distracters: weapons that can be projected to distract or confuse (e.g., dirt, gravel, hats, change, saliva).

- Shields: weapons used for protection from an attack (e.g., chairs, tables, trash can lids, cafeteria trays, books).

The examples provided are just that: examples. Almost anything that we come in contact with could probably fall into one or more of these categories. When dealing with a subject who may become violent, it is important for the officer to be aware of articles within the subject's immediate grasp and how they could be used. If possible, these articles should be removed from points of easy access or taken from the subject.

A way to heighten one's awareness of possible threats is to take a few minutes and reflect on what everyday objects could have been used to harm you during your last meeting with a subject. For example, as a police officer, were you standing too close to the teenager who held a pop bottle in his or her hand during an informal discussion? Or, as a penitentiary employee, did you move the telephone or letter opener off your desk before meeting with an inmate who was about to receive distressing news? While not intended to encourage paranoia, heightened awareness of one's surroundings is a simple self-defense strategy that requires no special training.

Weapons Made from Everyday Objects

While homemade weapons are probably of greater concern to the correctional officer than the police officer, the latter should also be conversant with these for the following reasons: (a) the inmate may have learned to manufacture these types of weapons before being incarcerated and may have carried them prior to incarceration; (b) having been exposed to these types of weapons while in prison, the released offender may feel more comfortable using them when back on the street; (c) the components, when disassembled, may not be illegal to possess and therefore the suspect carries them without fearing arrest. The suspect can then be armed in a matter of seconds if these articles are not removed. These homemade weapons usually fall within one of the following categories:

- Stabbing or cutting weapons: weapons with a sharp point or edge (e.g., picks and crude knives of various materials).

• Impact weapons: weapons of flexible or non-flexible composition used to bludgeon (e.g., pieces of pipe, small weight lifting bars, a solid weighted object placed in a sock, gloves or bags, crudely fashioned brass knuckles).
• Ligature weapons: weapons to impede the body's flow of oxygenated blood to the brain or oxygen to the lungs (e.g., garottes made from shoelaces).
• Projectile weapons: weapons which are thrown, launched, or fired (e.g., zip guns, homemade slingshots, articles that can spray irritating or noxious substances).

Since homemade weapons or variations on the above-mentioned examples are confiscated from lawbreakers inside and outside prison every day, a list of what has been devised would probably be out of date before it was published. Those officers who are interested in this subject should contact the person in their department who has been delegated the duty of compiling this information. Often, a description and picture are available and in some cases the articles themselves are retained for instructional purposes.

The ability to recognize articles which can be used as, or manufactured into, dangerous weapons, is a skill every officer should strive to attain. In the case of improvised weaponry, an ounce of prevention will go much further than the proverbial pound of cure.

Chapter 4

OFFICER SURVIVAL OF BLADED WEAPON ENCOUNTERS

Remember the last time you cut your finger. Hurt, didn't it? For a little cut, it sure did bleed, didn't it? Now picture yourself at the wrong end of a knife attack. Not a pretty thought, but one every law enforcement and correctional officer should give his or her attention to more than once in their career. To do so just might help keep it from becoming a reality, which is the goal of this chapter.

For the purposes of this chapter, "bladed weapons" can be defined as anything bearing an edge which can be used to injure by slashing. Usually, this means a knife, but it can also mean a machete, razor, hatchet, razor blade, or even an ice scraper. Many of these instruments can also be used in a stabbing fashion.

During the course of his or her career, the chances of a police officer encountering an individual armed with a bladed weapon are becoming less and less remote. According to the creators of the 1988 knife defense video, *Surviving Edged Weapons*, knife assaults on police officers rose 92 percent in the U.S. between 1978 and 1988. The cultural, demographic, and societal differences between other countries and the U.S. would indicate that these statistics are not comparable. However, criminals, being cut from the same cloth the world over, make the necessity for awareness of bladed weapons a must for any law enforcement official.

City bylaws prohibiting the sale of knives to young people or prohibiting the carrying of knives in licensed drinking establishments or public places have been attempted with varying degrees of success in Canada. Unfortunately, despite these forward-thinking pieces of legislation, there is still a glut of edged weapons being carried on a daily basis on the street.

Why is this the case? The primary reason, of course, is because a knife is both a weapon and a tool. This means, it can be legally carried on the street on the belt, or in the pocket in the case of a pocketknife.

Knives are also carried on the street because they are easier to conceal and generally easier to obtain than firearms. In Canada, most young offenders lack the financial resources or the criminal network to obtain even the crudest "Saturday night special." This may also be said of many adult offenders.

In Chapter 2 on gladiator schools, I alluded to why ex-offenders may choose a bladed weapon. In addition to the fact that for the offender on parole or probation a pocketknife can usually be carried without any negative sanction being imposed if discovered, ex inmates may also feel more comfortable with the knife because of their experience and familiarity with this weapon. This familiarity is usually acquired in a milieu where knife attacks and knife fighting are practiced and executed with chilling regularity: prison.

Recognition that bladed weapons are out on the street and may do harm to you or others may seem to be a premise too simple to mention. It is, however, a good place to start.

UNDERSTANDING THE WEAPON

One of the most disheartening aspects of teaching defense tactics to law enforcement personnel is the failure of some officers to recognize the lethal nature of edged weapons. Often, this leads to poor defense tactics on the officer's part or, worse yet, a cavalier approach to dealing with a knife attack. Both can be equally fatal.

I am routinely amazed by the number of officers who fail to remain physically fit or practise defense tactics once they leave their training academy. Furthermore, the percentage of officers who do not train in tactics to respond to a knife attack is even greater. At a knife defense seminar where I assisted in the teaching, only one police officer and one prisoner escort officer attended. This translated into less than 1 percent of the officers and staff employed by this fairly large urban police service. The reasons why officers fail to practice tactics which may prevent a potentially lethal encounter are numerous and are beyond the scope of this chapter.

Some correctional and police officers often fail to consider even a small edged weapon as dangerous. Prison incident reports have noted that an inmate can slice a correctional officer "from ear to ear" with a razor blade imbedded in a toothbrush. In one case where this happened and the officer survived, he has not returned to work in over two years.

TACTICS

Officers are often assaulted by edged weapons because they employ poor tactics when dealing with a potential attacker. Just who is a potential attacker? Simply put, it is anyone you come in contact with during the course of your shift.

There is a belief held by some police officers that because they are armed with a firearm, this will prevent them from being injured. The phrase "don't bring a knife to a gunfight" is often quoted by them to demonstrate their disdain for less than lethal tactics.

In the video, *Surviving Edged Weapons,* there is a demonstration of the minimum distance required between the officer and an attacker armed with a knife in order for the officer to successfully draw his or her weapon, fire two shots center mass and get out of the way of the onrushing knife wielder. The filmmakers calculate this distance to be approximately 21 feet. While the exact distance is debatable, the fact remains that if the officer is a few feet away from the suspect when a knife is pulled, there may not be sufficient time or space to successfully use a firearm to defend against the attack.

Another poor tactic often employed by police officers is to reach for their baton when they have left the baton in the patrol car, detachment locker, or at home. Many officers routinely fail to carry their batons with them while on patrol. Reasons cited for this behavior range from it being cumbersome when getting in and out of the patrol car, to a genuinely held fear that they will not be effective with it. Different baton systems (e.g., Koga, Lamb, PPCT, ASP, PR-24) can be investigated by officers who wish to enhance their skills with the baton.

A number of cities are using oleoresin capsicum (a cayenne pepper extract commonly referred to as capstun or pepper spray) as a tool to deal with bladed weapon attacks. When sprayed in the face of an attacker, it will usually inhibit breathing, induce coughing, and impair vision and motor control without residual effects. The benefit of such a tool is that it extends the distance from a suspect from which the officer can employ a defense tactic. It also provides officers with an alternative to using their firearms.

One should remember that the use of pepper spray should not be perceived as infallible. I remember seeing a picture that was published in the print media showing an officer having to wash his eyes after some capstun came in contact with them. A fellow officer had used this tool to disarm a knife-wielding woman. While the pepper spray had proved valuable to the officer who subsequently disarmed the woman, it might have been fatal to the other officer whose vision was impaired by it.

It is not my intention to provide the reader with a step-by-step manual of knife defense techniques. Study and practice with a qualified instructor in bladed weapon defense is far superior than trying to learn techniques from this chapter. One note of caution, however, may be appropriate at this juncture. You should critically assess the techniques taught by your martial arts instructor or police defense tactics trainer. One of the failings of certain martial arts or police defense courses is to teach defenses to knife attacks characterized by a single committed slash or thrust. Anyone who has viewed a knife attack or the results of one will attest that most often, such attacks are fluid and multi slash/thrust in nature.

Quality knife defense instruction should also cover attacks and defenses where the knife is held in various grips (e.g., ice pick, hammer), where the attack is delivered from various angles (e.g., horizontal, vertical, or diagonal stabs and slashes), methods of distraction, and the use of improvised weapons. Lastly, tactical options for dealing with knife threats while in the "hostage" position, up against a wall, or sitting down, are also invaluable to the officer.

A valuable training regime is to practice defensive techniques at full speed under close to real conditions. The use of a chalked practice weapon or magic markers (to leave evidence of potential wounds inflicted), goggles, protective equipment, and the wearing of your daily equipment is recommended here. While this does not come close to replicating the real thing, it will often demonstrate the difference between what can work and what can't. To enhance the reality factor, practice your techniques in varied lighting conditions and with the practice knife concealed until just before the attack begins. Lastly, once the necessary skills have been acquired, some practice should be done with a real bladed weapon. It should only be done under the supervision of a qualified instructor and with great care being given to safety.

Since we have discussed poor tactics, it is appropriate to focus on employing the proper defense tactics. The first thing to remember is that anyone you come into contact with may be armed. Without becoming paranoid, remember to keep an eye on the subject's hands at all times. Are the palms and fingertips in clear view? Are his or her hands in their pockets clutching a knife or "palming" one behind the forearm?

When the officer has to approach an individual, he or she should think and move tactically, remembering to stay out of the danger zone in front of the subject and inside the arms. The officer should watch the subject's demeanor for cues to aggressive action and for any friends or bystanders who may try to ambush the officer.

When searching an individual, an officer is at the greatest risk. At this range, the subject can strike, grab, stab, or slash. It is imperative to retain physical control of the suspect while searching. Ideally, hand-cuffs should be placed on the subject prior to any searching. Also, assume that the suspect has other weapons when one is found and complete the search.

The officer should be aware that suspects sometimes "booby trap" their clothing with razor blades and fishhooks to injure those who may search them. Therefore, extreme care should be taken. The officer should be cautious when putting his or her hands in pockets or over areas that cannot be visually inspected or probed with a pen or pencil. Kevlar gloves are now available to help prevent cuts and punctures while searching a suspect.

Lastly, with regard to searching, the officer should be cognizant of the dangers of conducting a "wall/prop" search (where the subject leans his or her hands against a wall or car during the search). A number of books have been written covering the inherent dangers of this type of search, most notably, the possibility of being disarmed, injured or killed.

WOUNDS AND THEIR TREATMENT

In his video, *Filipino Knife Fighting*, martial arts instructor Paul Vunak points out that most martial artists believe they can easily survive a cut on the forearm while disarming an adversary. Vunak challenges this approach to knife defense by slicing a side of meat to the bone with one slash. This graphically illustrates the drawback of attempting to disarm a knife fighter with any technique based on the acceptance of a cut. Acceptance of a cut, any cut, even a minor one, is not a good starting point for your defense tactics.

W.E. Fairbairn, co-creator of the Fairbairn-Sykes fighting knife (used by Allied Forces commandos) and former instructor at the Allied Forces World War II spy school, Camp X, includes in his book, *Get Tough*, a chart depicting the physiological effects of sustaining cuts. While this text is now over 50 years old, it does provide a quasi-scientific basis for the argument that a cut should be avoided at all costs. His chart shows that knife cuts can lead to loss of consciousness or life in a very short period of time.

It must be said, however, that there is a good chance during an altercation involving a knife that an officer will be cut. If you can't avoid being cut, your goal should be to try and receive the injury in a location where it will hurt you the least and allow you to gain a significant advantage. During a knife altercation, the officer should try to protect the following vital areas of the body: chest, neck, abdomen, groin, eyes, kidneys and femoral (thigh) artery.

Any forensic pathologist can verify that a victim of a knife attack will probably sustain "defensive" wounds to the hands and forearms prior to the final killing stroke being delivered. The officer should, if he or she is about to be cut on the forearms or hands, present the back of the forearms to the blade. This will prevent the blade from cutting tendons which permit the hands to grab. If these tendons are damaged, they will inhibit the officer from being able to use the hands to disarm the aggressor. If you are cut or stabbed during an attack, you should try to stop the bleeding by applying direct pressure to the wound. This may be possible only after the attack has been defended against successfully or has ceased. It should be remembered that with some cuts, consciousness can be lost very quickly.

If a limb has been cut, it should be raised above the level of the heart to inhibit the flow of blood. If you are unable to apply direct pressure to the wound (e.g., you are lying on the ground and can't use you arms), roll over onto the wound and allow your body weight to apply pressure. In the event that a bladed weapon has been left impaled in the body, do not try to remove it, as its presence may be impeding the flow of blood. A punctured lung should be covered with plastic or some other non-porous material to help prevent its collapse.

After being cut, you should try to slow down your breathing. This will correspondingly slow down your heartbeat and with it, the rate of bleeding. As well, as soon as possible, you should radio your dispatcher for assistance and request transport to a medical facility. Your exact location should be immediately given in the event that you lose consciousness. Lastly, after sustaining a knife injury, do not lose your desire to survive.

EQUIPMENT

There are various items of police equipment, other than the firearm or baton, which may enable an officer to survive a knife attack. The bullet-resistant Kevlar vest has been shown to offer protection against slashes to the body and some stabbing attacks. Some vests have pockets where metal "trauma" plates can be inserted. These plates enhance the vest's ability to protect against stabbing attacks. In addition to Kevlar vests, Kevlar gloves and wrist-to-elbow sleeves are now available for purchase.

A knife attack-resistant vest is presently being marketed in Britain. The "Anti Knife Jacket" is designed to be worn under the shirt and offers protection against knife attacks. The anti-knife insert has lightweight lamellar metal sections fronting the Kevlar packs at the front and back of the jacket.

The officer's radio, clipboard, ticket book, and articles of his or her uniform (e.g., jacket or hat) may also be used to prevent injury by a knife. As indicated in the previous chapter, almost any object can be used by the officer as a shield to keep the weapon away—that is, if the "shield" is in hand when the attack begins.

PUTTING IT ALL TOGETHER

The successful defense to any type of attack begins with awareness. If one can spot a potential attack and neutralize it before it is initiated, then the need to rely on physical tactics is diminished.

The second key to success is the use of appropriate tactics. This covers tactical movement, angling, application of joint locks and handcuffs, as well as armed and unarmed physical responses to attacks. If these tactics are not learned under the supervision of a qualified instructor and practiced on a regular basis, then their chances of success are greatly diminished.

The third key to success is physical conditioning. Without staying in good physical condition (through regular aerobic/anaerobic, strength, flexibility, and hand speed training), your chances of surviving a knife attack are severely reduced.

The final key to success is mental attitude. When I was about 12 years old, my Karate instructor told me: "If you do not fear the knife, the knife will not cut you." For over 25 years, I have been unable to discern whether this ancient saying is a pearl of wisdom or a blueprint for disaster. While it is clear that a healthy concern for the knife is a good thing, this should not paralyze the officer when a bladed weapon is pulled out or cause him or her to react in a purely defensive way.

Visual imaging practice on how you will react to a knife attack will enhance both your physical skills (a proven sports psychology theory) and your ability to achieve a proper mental attitude when attacked with a bladed weapon.

Lastly, with regard to mental attitude, development of the mental toughness to continue fighting and not give up after sustaining an injury is very important.

Chapter 5

ENHANCEMENT OF RESTRAINT TECHNIQUES

Joint locks, come-alongs, and pain compliance techniques are defensive tactics maneuvers used to control an individual, allow you to apply handcuffs, or move the individual securely from one place to another. Unless specification is required, I will use the term "restraint techniques" in a generic sense to cover the various types of holds detailed below.

This chapter will not teach you specific techniques but, rather, offers information which will enhance the techniques and tactics you were taught at your training academy. If your academy courses did not cover this material or you do not remember what you were taught, hopefully this chapter will encourage you to seek appropriate training.

From a defensive tactics perspective, it is important that you learn how to use effective restraint techniques and have backup techniques if they should fail. When you are involved in a stressful situation and without such knowledge and skills, you may escalate to a higher, and perhaps inappropriate, level of response on the force continuum either because you do not feel comfortable using a lock, it fails, or you become fatigued.

The number of times that you will actually have to use force during an arrest or to move an individual from a cell is not as frequent as you may think, however, not everyone comes along quietly. During your career as a police or correctional officer you will encounter three types of individuals. You have the "no" people who will not cooperate with you, the "yes" people who will cooperate with you, and the "maybe" people who are still deciding whether to cooperate or are mildly unco-operative. For a violently resisting "no" person, the application of restraint techniques alone may not be an appropriate response. The reason is that they usually cannot be applied without, as renowned martial arts instructor Dan Inosanto terms it, "tranquillizing" the body of the individual first. What tranquillization techniques are and how they are applied will be discussed later.

As with any defensive tactics, prior to using them on the job, you should know the applicable laws of your jurisdiction and appropriate force policy concerning when and which different levels of force can be applied to effect an arrest.

JOINT LOCKS, PAIN COMPLIANCE TECHNIQUES, AND COME-ALONGS

Joint locks can be defined as restraint techniques that cause pain to a joint through pressure, torsion or hyper-extension of the joint. Pain compliance techniques are those techniques which force a person to comply by introducing pain. This can be through something as simple as a hair pull or by stimulating the nerves of the subject through pressure exerted by a digit or limb. A variation of this theme is to gain control by causing a temporary motor dysfunction of an individual through striking techniques to a pressure point, e.g., a kick to the femoral nerve in the leg. Come-alongs are joint locks or pain compliance techniques that enable an officer to move someone from one place to another; the person "comes along" with you. However, I am not referring here to merely leading someone by the arm in the guise of being in control.

Pressure point striking techniques can be an effective backup technique when other restraint techniques fail for a variety of reasons: loss of grip when hand or arms are slick, the presence of bulky clothing or gloves, or an individual with a very high threshold of pain tolerance.

In addition to uses against "maybe" and "no" people (once a certain degree of violence has been defused), restraint techniques can be useful against passive resisters and people who anchor themselves to objects and refuse to let go. Your force policy should be consulted, however, regarding the application of such techniques against passive resisters prior to their use.

The most important thing to remember is that restraint techniques are only a temporary means of restraining someone. At an appropriate time, you should make use of your handcuffs to secure the individual after you have used a restraint technique.

Handcuffing and Locks

According to Pressure Point Control Tactics (PPTC) Management Systems, a St. Louis, Missouri, law enforcement training organization, an independent, unpublished study conducted by the St. Louis City Police Department revealed that 67 percent of resistance from a subject occurred when the first handcuff was secured on a subject's wrist. For this reason, when applying handcuffs, you will want to control the individual through the use of a restraint technique so that you will be able to secure the second handcuff and won't end up fighting someone who is swinging the dangling handcuff as an improvised weapon.

Various speedcuffing courses are available, if you have not already been exposed to these techniques at the academy. These courses, in addition to speedy application of the handcuffs, also teach excellent takedowns which will assist you in gaining control of a resisting subject.

Tactical Communication in Relation to Restraint Techniques

Why tactical communication in relation to restraint techniques? Because the purpose of any restraint technique is to effect control, we should examine the easiest way to achieve this control: voluntary compliance after a verbal request is made.

Much has been written in police circles about taking control of the situation upon arrival at the scene and giving authoritative directions. This approach is generally true but must be tempered with common sense. Be professional and polite. Avoid profanity and verbal jousting. You can be in control without being demeaning. Don't let your ego force you into an unwanted physical confrontation. It is easier to talk someone into the car than to wrestle them in later.

If appropriate, ask the individual his or her first name, and if you can, use it. Ask what the problem is. For those who disagree with this "social worker" approach, remember that from a tactical point of view a person is less likely to be able to respond quickly when thinking of an answer. Remember though, when engaging in any dialogue, the subject might be trying to lull you into being off guard.

Most communication between individuals is non verbal, therefore, understand that your posture and demeanor, as well as your verbal directions, are sending messages. A confident demeanor sends a message that you are confident in your abilities; trying to intimidate someone sends another message and may not elicit the cooperation you are looking for.

When speaking to someone, don't stand too close unless you are moving in to effect a technique. There are two reasons for this. First, you are violating his or her personal space which can trigger a violent response. Second, if you are too close, you will not have sufficient reaction time to counter a sudden attack. Also, do not stand in front of the individual, exposing the vital areas of your body. Approach from the side of the individual. As most people are right-handed you may want to approach his or her right side, so that you can tie up the person's strongest hand.

I am a firm believer in making non-threatening motions with the hands while talking. "Talking with the hands" puts them in a position where it is easier to block or effect a stunning technique. When gesturing, though, you should avoid pointing your finger, touching or poking the individual, clenching or shaking your fist, or putting your palm forward in a stop position. These gestures often elicit negative responses from people.

When you are applying or have applied a restraint technique, give loud, simple, verbal directions one at a time. If you confuse or frustrate a person who is suffering pain, you may cause a sudden influx of adrenalin which can enhance his or her strength and pain tolerance and render your restraint useless. I will elaborate on this point in the next chapter.

Lastly, regarding communication, your partner should know what code words you will be using which alert him or her that you will be effecting a takedown or restraint technique. Former British and Canadian police officer and author Gary Foo suggests in his book *Tactical Communications* a question along the lines of: "Is there anything I can do that will cause you to come along quietly?" Anything short of compliance will result in both officers immediately escalating higher up on the force continuum to gain control. You should also spend time discussing with your partner what type of tactics or techniques you might use, and give your partner verbal directions during the application of the techniques, e.g., "Partner, pin the other hand!" This avoids working counter-productively.

Problems with the Application of Traditional Techniques

Most self-defense systems, even those that are primarily striking or weapons oriented rather than grappling-based, have some restraint element in them. Japanese Judo, Ju-Jitsu, Aikido, Chinese Chin-Na, Korean Wharang-do, Hapkido, Filipino Dumog, Indonesian Silat and Western wrestling are the most common martial arts that feature these techniques and counters to them. Unfortunately, officers often have difficulty applying the restraint techniques found in these martial arts systems and other defensive tactics systems.

The primary reason that restraint techniques do not work, as alluded to earlier, is that officers rely on sheer strength to put on the restraint and do not tranquillize the individual. If your opponent is large and/or strong, he or she may just muscle out of your restraint using arm strength alone if you do not use the tranquillizers to be discussed later.

As noted earlier, pain tolerance, a sweaty hold, or the presence of bulky clothes or gloves can inhibit proper technique application when you attempt to apply your restraint hold, as can the influence of alcohol or drugs. Physiological factors such as the size of the officer's hand versus the size of the opponent's body part being restrained also affect technique application. For example, it would be inappropriate for a smaller officer to attempt an elbow/shoulder restraint on a larger individual when a finger or wrist restraint might be more effective.

One sure way to get injured when applying a restraint technique is to attempt a technique during a stressful incident which requires a high degree of fine motor control. During a high-stress encounter, fine motor skill is usually lost; therefore, any techniques taught should be simple and use gross motor skills.

Many individuals know counters to the various restraint techniques taught to police. You can go far to foil these counters by following one simple rule—don't forget about the person's other hand (or knee, foot, or head). Do not expose your vital targets when you have applied a restraint because you may still be vulnerable to a counter applied with the unrestrained hand (e.g., eye pokes, punches). A verbal direction for the subject to put his or her hand behind the head might be sufficient to prevent that sucker punch.

Lastly, watch out for faked compliance when a restraint technique is applied. Often, officers ease up on the pressure of a hold when they hear, "I give up" or resistance ceases. You can and should maintain control or pressure without hurting the individual.

General Principles Concerning the Enhanced Application of Techniques

As I said earlier, the purpose of this chapter is not to teach specific restraint techniques, nor do I propose to tell you when to apply a restraint. Each situation you will encounter is different, and no hard and fast rules apply. As well, once you have applied a restraint technique, it may be up to you to defend the decision you have made to move up the force continuum to use these techniques. What I will offer are some general principles which may enhance your ability to apply restraint techniques.

First of all, think and act tactically while doing your job. You should not be responding to any incident, no matter how routine, on automatic pilot. Once, when stopped by a traffic officer in the town where I reside, I tested just how untactical the local police were. As soon as I had pulled over, I exited my vehicle and went up and stuck my smiling face in the window of the officer's cruiser and engaged in a casual conversation. During the course of the traffic stop, I stayed within arm's reach of the officer with my right hand stuck in my coat pocket. To correct these tactical errors on the officer's part, I later shared this experience with the officer's defensive tactics instructor who was a fellow martial arts student at the time.

I mentioned previously that it is often difficult to apply a restraint technique without tranquillizing the body. By tranquillizing the body, what we mean is the application of pain or distraction/misdirection (feint or ruse) to prevent the subject from launching a counterattack while you move in to apply the technique.

In combat there are a number of ranges: weapons range (the longest range is for firearms, shorter for batons or knives), kicking range, punching range, trapping range, and grappling range. Attempts at applying a restraint technique on a non-willing participant in the gym will quickly demonstrate that it is virtually impossible to close the distance from the punching/kicking range to the grappling range unscathed without preceding your entry with tranquillization. Striking techniques to various nerves is one way of tranquillizing using pain. Distraction techniques range from throwing something in the subject's face (e.g., a notebook), to effecting the technique in the middle of a sentence.

Another general principle is that control is an all-or-nothing proposition. If you don't have total control of an individual when you effect a restraint technique, you do not have any control. It is only a matter of time before the person who is not being adequately controlled launches an effective counterattack. A good way of telling whether you have control is that when you have applied sufficient force when using a restraint, most people will raise up on their toes.

There is a never-ending debate concerning where you should look when confronting an individual. One school of thought is that if you don't look them in the eyes you are demonstrating a lack of control. The other school of thought, which I call "tactical vision," is that you should look at a subject's chest so that your peripheral vision can scan any movements of hands or feet. A blending of these two schools is appropriate. When you have sufficient space between you and the individual, look into his or her eyes, but don't lock in—remember to keep their hands in view. When you are moving in to effect a technique, use "tactical vision."

When applying a restraint technique, do not engage in a battle of strength to get it secured. When you find yourself wrestling for a technique, you should go to something else—either disengage or upset his or her balance using a takedown, or escalate to higher level of force (e.g., hard hand techniques, impact weapon, pepper spray).

It has been my experience that when most people wrestle, they forget that they can also employ strikes. One possible reason for this is because these strikes are not crisp power shots. However, depending on the circumstances, the use of a head butt or knee strike might be appropriate and sufficient to apply the restraint. When you are in grappling range, you should also be aware that groin or eye gouges, tearing techniques and biting can be used against you (or by you if circumstances are appropriate).

As a general principle, be very cautious of restraint techniques which rely on impact tools. Those officers who have received training with the PR-24 are aware that this impact tool can be used to apply restraints. It is my opinion, and that of others, that this fine motor control skill may be too hard to accomplish during an altercation. I am not an advocate of the school of thought that impact weapons should only be used as impact weapons, but you should evaluate your comfort level with these techniques prior to actual use in the field.

Finally, with regard to general principles, make sure you know weapon-retention techniques if your firearm is grabbed and weapon-disarming techniques if your firearm, flashlight, impact weapon, or pepper spray canister are taken away from you during an incident. Also, you should know your force's policy regarding the use of back-up weapons.

Multiple-Attacker Situations

The martial art of Aikido practices defenses against multiple attacks which use joint locks as a defence. The joint locks are used to quickly lock and take down or lock and push one individual into another. This type of response to multiple attacks demands a high skill level that you may not be able to replicate during a high stress street confrontation without years of training and practice.

It is almost impossible to safely secure a restraint technique when you are dealing with more than one individual. You should become familiar with dynamic striking techniques that will temporarily incapacitate the individual you are dealing with if a greater threat becomes apparent (e.g., you're wrestling with subject #1 and subject #2 attacks you with a knife). You should also explore the following tactical options to deal with multiple attackers.

Putting one individual in front of the other as an obstacle or shield so you don't have to deal with more than one at a time is the first rule. Don't let them circle you or clutch onto you are the second and third rules.

A simple exercise which both illustrates the dangers of multiple opponents and is good practice is to have an individual playing the role of an assailant that you have struck hold onto your leg while you try to defend against another attacker. I can't claim ownership of this training scenario as it comes from an individual who noted that this aspect, from the bar fight scene in the Humphrey Bogart movie, *Treasure of Sierra Madre*, is close to what can happen in a real fight.

Lastly, do not neglect to use you peripheral vision or take a quick look around when dealing with one subject so that you do not get blindsided by a friend or accomplice of the person you are subduing.

Training Exercises and Practice

Any training to hone your restraint technique skill should attempt to be realistic. You should try to apply a lock on your training partner when he or she doesn't want you to and is resisting. Without tranquillization techniques, you will quickly see that this is difficult to do, especially if your partner is big, strong, tough, and trained, and that you will become tired very quickly. While making sure your training is realistic, remember to pay attention to safety. Leave your ego outside the training room. Many macho individuals who routinely refuse to "tap out" (indicating a restraint has been fully applied and that the pressure to the joint should cease) eventually end up in the emergency room. You should try to practice your techniques the same way every time so that they become ingrained, working with your firearm side away from the subject.

Regarding the talking hands tactic I mentioned earlier, practice your strikes from the talking hands position and also from down around your waist. Sometimes raising your hands alerts the individual of your intentions and you will have to keep your hands down. Sports which reinforce quick hands such as table tennis can be used to cross train striking skills.

You may wish to explore the martial arts of Filipino Dumog and shootwrestling which contain "lock flow" training. This involves switching from one lock to another. This training technique enhances the ability to flow from one restraint to another and provides a sequence to practice your repertoire of techniques. It is not intended to make you the master of many restraints, as this could confuse you in an altercation. You only need a few key restraints you can use interchangeably, if one does not work, and you do not wish to escalate to a higher level.

You may also wish to explore Silat, mentioned in Chapter 1, as this art contains a number of devastating takedowns that can be used to augment your restraint training. The hand-trapping techniques of Wing Chun Gung Fu might also be explored to enhance your restraint training. In addition, do not forget your multiple-attacker, high-stress training. If you really want to get an idea what fighting a number of attackers is really like, suit up in some protective padding and go all out for a couple of minutes. Using this training, you will soon learn how fast exhaustion sets in and just how bad a situation can become.

Lastly, you may wish to train your grip strength, as this is an attribute used often in grappling. In addition, grip strength will provide better control when firing heavier-caliber automatic pistols. One great exercise which simulates grabbing on while grappling is to get a hand squeezer and hold it in the squeezed position for 2 to 3 minutes. Increase the time you can squeeze if this is too easy, or put a penny between the handles and don't drop it.

A Few Final Thoughts

Earlier, when discussing problems associated with the application of restraint techniques, I failed to mention the primary reason why they do not work in a real-life situation. Restraint techniques often fail in the field because officers fail to train them until they are mastered, and they subsequently maintain that level of expertise. You probably would not qualify one time with your service firearm and then never practice with it, yet most officers fail to train the restraint techniques they will use more often than their firearms.

One final comment—after an arrest has been made and a control hold has been applied, a good rule of thumb is to ask the subject if they need medical attention and then document the request, the time it was made, and response. The reasons for this are obvious from both a legal and humanitarian perspective. As a professional, it is your job to use the least amount of force to effect an arrest, and should the subject be injured in the scuffle, it is incumbent on you to obtain medical intervention, even if he or she has just tried to take your head off.

Chapter 6

HANDCUFFING TIPS FOR PROFESSIONALS

Often while watching reality-based police television programs, like "Cops" or "American Detective," one of the funniest aspects is when officers detain and attempt to search an individual before handcuffing that person. It is humorous because frequently while the search is being done, the detainee takes off running with several officers, laden down with radios, flashlights, heavy boots and other equipment, in hot (albeit slow and exhausting) foot pursuit. What is not so humorous is that sometimes the detainee chooses the violent option of the "flight or fight" response and officers are injured or killed.

Unfortunately, in my opinion, an insufficient amount of time is spent on teaching, reviewing, or practicing handcuffing techniques, either during recruit or in-service training. This is unfortunate because officers will use their handcuffs every time an arrest is made (depending on their organization's policies). A greater amount of time is spent on handgun training and yearly requalification. While it is obvious that the lethal nature of the service firearm demands a high degree of expertise, it should be remembered that some officers go through their whole careers without ever having to draw their firearm in the line of duty. They will, however, probably use their handcuffs in the course of the majority of their arrests.

Handcuffing Psychology

In one study done in the Austin, Texas, area and reported in the *Texas Police Journal*, almost 65 percent of assaults on officers were in retaliation to the police officers attempt to apply handcuffs to the suspect. In the previous chapter, I mentioned the study conducted by the St. Louis City Police Department which revealed that 67 percent of resistance from a subject occurred when the first handcuff was secured on the subject's wrist. Such statistics point to the need for officers to master the use of handcuffs to ensure they go home safely after their shift.

There are a number of reasons why people do not want to be handcuffed. They may feel they cannot adequately defend themselves from abuse by the arresting officers, or they may feel that they have lost their dignity when handcuffs are applied. However, I feel the primary reason why people become violent when handcuffs are applied is because their application implies a sense of finality to the situation. Detainees realize they cannot talk the officer out of this course of action, that they will not be getting off with a warning, and that they will probably be going to jail.

PPCT founder Bruce Siddle feels that a suspect's reaction time is often slowed down with the consumption of alcohol. An arrested subject may not realize the totality of the situation until after the first handcuff is applied. However, before the second handcuff is applied, the reality of the arrest sets in and the subject resists. Siddle also notes that when dealing with experienced criminals, they will resist in one of two fashions: by being totally uncooperative, both physically and verbally, or by waiting for an opportune moment. That moment may be before the second handcuff is applied.

Finally, Mr. Siddle points out that a study done by Elizabeth Croft indicated that resistance to arrest usually occurs at the moment of "touch." Therefore, when the officer has decided to handcuff the individual, control has to be taken at the moment of initial physical contact and should be retained until the subject is no longer a potential threat. This is accomplished through the use of any restraint technique that will allow the officer to be able to secure the second handcuff without potentially having to fight someone who is swinging the dangling handcuff as an improvised weapon.

Knowing When to Handcuff

Should the officer apply handcuffs for every arrest? From a defensive tactics perspective, I would recommend that handcuffs always be used prior to a search. However, the officer should be conversant with departmental policy on the use of handcuffs, as this should dictate whether handcuffing prior to arresting is permissible. The police service's policy should also delineate when discretion can be exercised concerning the use of handcuffs after an arrest.

If there are any doubts, I recommend that the officer err on the side of safety. Remember, this decision will affect not only the officer's safety but also the safety of the public, fellow officers and the suspect–who may be tempted to flee or fight if uncuffed. The arresting officer will not know whether or not the simple shoplifter he or she has arrested is actually a violent offender who will do anything to go free, as was the case in 1985, when suspected mass murderer Charles Ng pulled a gun when he was arrested in Calgary for shoplifting food. Therefore, the officer should not be lulled by a docile manner or the relatively minor nature of the call.

Handcuffing should take place before the officer searches an individual. Handcuffing prior to a search will protect the officer from being ambushed by an individual who has practiced countermeasures to be used during a search. For those readers who may think such concerns are paranoiac, video-surveillance cameras in various prisons have captured inmates practicing just such techniques.

Officers should be conversant with their service's policy concerning whether they can handcuff an injured, handicapped or apparently-dead suspect. Remember, such persons may be armed with hidden weapons, or may not be as disabled as they would appear, and may still be able to cause injury.

Knowing Where to Place the Handcuffs on the Detainee

Handcuffs should be applied with the detainee's arms behind the back. This prevents them from being used as weapons, which will be discussed later. However, putting the handcuffs on the detainee with the arms in front is better than not putting them on at all. Also, with respect to placement of the handcuffs, officers should never handcuff the person to an object or to themselves. This could prove injurious to the detainee or the officer.

Applying Handcuffs

Officers can only apply handcuffs if they remember to carry them and can reach them when required. They should be carried in an accessible location on the duty belt. This should be the same location all the time so that the officer will remember where to reach for them when under stress. Make sure the location you choose is comfortable and does not cause back problems. One position which may cause back problems is to position the carrying case directly in line with the spine. If the officer falls on his or her back, serious injury to the spine may occur.

Officers should practice retrieving and gripping the handcuffs in the proper position for handcuffing without having to look at them. Handcuff with the weapon side away from the suspect, maintaining a safe distance from the individual until an opportune moment to close the distance, gain control and apply the handcuffs arises. Always do a visible check for weapons before entering the reactionary gap. If resistance is encountered during handcuffing, the officer has the options of disengaging or escalating up the force continuum to gain control. One tactic to use which may help you from having to escalate in force is to have the suspect look away from you when you are entering to handcuff. This prevents the suspect from knowing when to execute a surprise counterattack.

The easiest way to apply handcuffs is when there is compliance. Therefore, officers should seek the path of least resistance during an arrest and try to apply the handcuffs with the compliance of the detainee.

The handcuffs must be applied when the suspect is under control. Control should not be confused with the semblance of control one observes when seeing an officer lightly grasping a suspect by the arm during an arrest, as mentioned in the previous chapter. Control is an all-or-nothing proposition and is not proportionate to whether detainees will allow themselves to be handcuffed peacefully or not. In all cases, a secure hold to control the individual should be applied. Remember, a seemingly peaceful subject can become violent at any time. Also, watch out when putting the subject's two hands close together to apply the second handcuff, as he or she can use the free hand to break your hold.

Exercising control, however, does not give an officer the licence to use excessive force. Leaving aside the possible legal and medical implications of using such questionable practices as slapping a suspect's wrists with the ratcheted arm of handcuffs, from a tactical perspective, such tactics can cause a subject to attempt to break free of the officer's control.

For those who require a more vivid picture as to why undue force should not be employed, I offer the following physiological tidbit. An excessive amount of pain caused to an individual can result in the adrenal glands dumping excessive amounts of adrenaline in the body. Adrenaline in these amounts can result in suspects being impervious to further pain, doubling their strength, or both. Nor should control be given up too soon, either. Just because a detainee is handcuffed does not mean that he or she cannot become violent. This control should be maintained until the suspect has been thoroughly searched, handcuffed, and placed in a secure facility. Handcuffs are a temporary measure until the detainee can be placed in a secure facility. Remember, people have bitten through or snapped handcuffs while under the influence of drugs like PCP. So do not relax your guard simply because your prisoner is handcuffed.

Speedcuffing

It goes without saying the quicker one can apply both the handcuffs, the less chance one risks being bonked on the head with the second. Various speedcuffing courses are available, if officers have not already been exposed to these techniques at the academy. These courses, in addition to speedy application of the handcuffs (approximately 3 seconds) also teach excellent takedowns that will assist in gaining control of a resisting subject.

Handcuffs as Weapons

As stated earlier, one should always control the handcuffed suspect. Handcuffs do not fully immobilize a prisoner. So do not think that someone is not a threat simply because they have been handcuffed. Handcuffs can be used as weapons either against an officer who ends up struggling with a suspect who is handcuffed or by the officer who has been taken hostage and handcuffed.

The worst position to end up in when struggling with a suspect whose hands are handcuffed in front of him or her is when this individual has circled your neck. When the suspect is in front of you, this position is similar to a clinch position in boxing or wrestling. Not only can the suspect drive knee strikes into the officer's stomach, groin, and thighs, he or she can also effect strangulation techniques. This situation is made worse when the suspect is behind the officer. In this position, the handcuffs serve as an improvised garrotte. Even when the suspect does not have hold of the officer's neck when the handcuffs are in front, he or she can still effect a number of offensive techniques. The suspect can club with the metal handcuffs, throw a two-fisted punch, strike with the elbows, poke or gouge at the eyes, pull hair, or execute a headlock, throw, or restraint technique.

In case the reader may believe that the situation might be safer if detainees' hands are handcuffed behind their backs, think again! In addition to head butts, shoulder butts, knee strikes, kicks, and foot stomps, the suspect can also bite and even use that good old Canadian hip check technique. Anyone who has played ice hockey and has been on the receiving end of a hip check to the groin or thigh can attest to the pain associated with this technique.

If the officer has his or her handcuffs in hand and is forced to escalate to a higher level on the force continuum to make an arrest, using the handcuffs as improvised weapons can help subdue the suspect. Should the suspect throw punches or kicks, the handcuffs can be used to block these techniques. This is a variation of the FMA concept of "defanging the snake," in essence, inflicting pain against the fist, foot or shin of the attacker to prevent the continuation of these actions.

The handcuffs can be used as a number of other improvised weapons. They can be a makeshift set of brass knuckles. With this use, the locking mechanism of the handcuffs should be in the palm of the hand. Otherwise, the officer could potentially crush his or her fingers if the handcuffs closed when executing a punch. The handcuffs can also be used as other weapons, such as an improvised palm sap against bony parts of the body or a set of improvised "tiger claws" for ripping techniques. They can also be used in a manner similar to a number of projectile weapons such as Argentinean *bolos* or Japanese throwing stars. They can also serve as improvised flailing weapons similar to the Japanese *nunchaku* or medieval morning star (a spiked ball connected to a stick by a length of chain). Clearly, such techniques should only be used to prevent life-threatening assaults.

One non-lethal weapon that most police officers are familiar with is the Persuader or Kubotan. Handcuffs can be used as an improvised

Persuader or Kubotan by applying pressure to cause pain to the detainee where his or her bones are close to the surface, e.g., between fingers, on top of the hand, along the ribs, sternum, clavicle, spine, wrist, shoulder blade, or dug into flesh (muscles, kidney, groin). Lastly, the improvised Persuader/Kubotan can be used as a pain compliance assistance tool to pinch an ear or nose.

Pain Compliance Techniques

Handcuffs can be used as a pain compliance tool when they have been applied on the detainee by turning the edge of the handcuff into the wrist bones, thereby causing pain. The officer, as a professional, should be careful not to misuse this technique to abuse a detainee.

Sometimes when arresting a suspect, this individual will adopt the "turtle" position. Here, the individual curls up into a ball, with his or her arms tucked in and so as not to give up the hands for cuffing. Pressure point control tactics can be used in these instances. Such techniques usually involve fingertip pressure applied to various nerve bundles located on the neck or head. For those officers who are hesitant to put their hands near the suspect's mouth or are hesitant to use pressure points on the head or neck, other pain compliance techniques can be used to force detainees to give up their wrists for handcuffing.

In addition to the old standby police technique of twisting the sensitive skin of the inner thigh, the new Japanese ring sport of shootfighting (a combination of kicking, punching and submission hold wrestling) offers such variations as kneeling on the Achilles tendon or digging the elbow along the side of the spine.

Takedowns

Takedowns using handcuffs can be used both by the police officer to help effect an arrest or against the officer by a detainee who is familiar with countermeasures to foil arrest techniques. PPCT teaches officers to pull on the unattached handcuff to induce pain to the detainee's wrist, causing him or her to adopt a prone position which facilitates the placement of the second handcuff.

Criminals teach other criminals that when handcuffs are applied in the front, the chain can be wrapped around the wrist or fingers and a takedown can be effected against a police officer.

Improvised and Hidden Keys

Once the officer has put the handcuffs on the detainee, the next thing is to search the individual. This is done for a number of reasons. First, the officer will want to make sure the individual does not have a hidden weapon. Second, the officer will want to ensure that the individual does not have the means to defeat the restraints just put on his or her wrists, specifically, that they do not have any real or improvised handcuff keys hidden on their person.

Improvised keys can be fashioned from a number of everyday articles, such as pens or pieces of metal or plastic. Real handcuff keys can be concealed on the person (e.g., taped under a belt or watchband, hidden inside seams of clothes, secreted in a wallet or matchbook, or placed under a bandage). As well, they can be concealed inside the body of a detainee (e.g., placed in the mouth or anus or, as in one Canadian case mentioned earlier, taped inside the belly button).

In addition to thoroughly searching a detainee for keys, a number of actions can be taken to avoid handcuffs being picked. For example, duct tape can be taped around the holes. As well, the hands can be cuffed in back with holes turned toward the body and the palms of the hands facing outward, as this makes it more difficult for the suspect to use his or her fingers to pick or unlock the handcuffs.

Transporting Prisoners

After detainees have been thoroughly searched for hidden weapons and keys, they should be placed in the back of the police cruiser. If there is no protective screen between the officer and the detainee, care should be taken to ensure that he or she is not directly behind the driver, unless another officer is sitting beside the detainee. This will prevent him or her from attempting to slip the handcuffs over their hips to the front where they can be used to garrotte the driver.

While moving your prisoner to the car, remember to be vigilant against surprise attack by friends or accomplices of the individual. If attacked by others while bringing the detainee to the car, one tactical option is to sweep out the legs of the individual. This leaves the officer free to deal with attackers without having to worry about the detainee taking a free shot while the officer is distracted.

Two final commonsense points with respect to transporting prisoners that are handcuffed: first, ensure that the detainee has on the seat belt. This will inhibit any attempts to remove the handcuffs and will prevent injury if the driver has to unexpectedly apply the brakes. Second, when removing a detainee from the patrol car, watch out for that surprise kick. Approach the detainee from side farthest away from his or her feet.

When the Police Officer Is Taken Hostage

What can the officer do when taken hostage by someone and secured with handcuffs? If the person has the officer put on the hand-cuffs in front, the officer can mislead them into believing that the handcuffs are being secured by making the ratchet sound by dragging the arm along the metal. This deception continues with the officer holding the handcuffs in place until attempting a countermove.

If the person has put on the handcuffs, the officer will have to rely on a spare key secreted on his or her person. Some trainers suggest the best location is directly above the ankle where it can be reached if one is handcuffed in front or in back. One word of caution for American officers about choosing this location–the key will probably be found by a suspect looking for an ankle holster for a backup weapon. Taping the key to the inside of your boot or shoe might overcome this draw-back.

Other Special Situations

How do you prevent detainees from slipping the handcuffs over their hips so that their hands end up in front? The ability to do this is not as simple as it looks, such as shown in a movie scene a few years ago where a fleeing suspect jumped on the hood of a car and, as he jumped off, passed the handcuffs to the front. It is possible, however, especially by persons of smaller stature or those with narrow hips and long arms. Slipping the handcuffs through the detainee's belt avoids this problem, as does use of a rappeller's D ring. Also, pulling the individual's shirt or coat down below the shoulders so that his or her arm movements are restricted may inhibit escape attempts.

People with slim wrists may also be able to slide handcuffs off their arms. Therefore, if the person has small wrists, you can cross the wrists over, or place the wrists together and then put on the handcuff. Use the other handcuff to secure the restraints to their belt or belt loop. If the person is very large, you may have to link two sets of handcuffs together.

If you have special concerns (such as not being confident that you can safely put on the handcuffs or that the detainee might attempt to run) or are waiting for backup, have the detainee lie down or sit down. Having the detainee kneel down has fallen into some disfavor in defensive tactics training because some offenders practise locking up and flipping the arresting officer from this position. Lastly, if the prisoner must be handcuffed in the front because he or she is injured or cannot bend their arms behind their back for other reasons, pass the handcuffs through a belt, if one is being worn, and buckle it in the back.

Multiple Subjects

If there are multiple subjects, they should be positioned so that one individual is between the other(s) and the officer. This is done so that the first person to be handcuffed and searched can be used as a shield or can be pushed into the other(s) to buy the officer some time to use an appropriate tactical response if ambushed. When positioning them in such a manner, the officer should not allow his or her view to be obstructed. This will insure that if any of the detainees reaches for a hidden weapon or hides evidence, this will be seen.

If the officer is dealing with multiple subjects and only has one set of handcuffs, the officer should handcuff the right hands of the subjects together. This causes them to be off balance and makes it difficult for them to coordinate their movements. If the officer is afraid they will run, handcuff the wrist of one to the ankle of the other. They may run, but they won't get far. This technique, however, should be cleared with respect to departmental policy.

Removing the Cuffs

The handcuffs should be removed only when the detainee has been thoroughly searched and will not injure anyone, including themselves. Do not assume that a person has been searched just because he or she has been turned over in handcuffs by another officer. That other officer might not have had time, or might have forgotten, to search the individual. Every officer should take the time to search every individual turned over to their custody.

Civil Litigation Avoidance

As indicated earlier, each officer should be conversant with their police service's handcuff policy and follow it. Be aware that some persons, when restrained, can die due to sudden death syndrome, a sudden fatal reaction to being restrained. Therefore, officers should always be prepared to explain why the handcuffs were applied. A good practice is also to record this reason in arrest notes, along with the time when the handcuffs were applied and removed. Another often neglected practice is to double-lock the handcuffs. Double-locking the cuffs keeps them from being tightened by the arrestee who could then bring suit or complaint against the officer.

When applying the handcuffs, the officer should explain to the person that they are being applied for the safety of both parties. Providing a reason can possibly defuse hostility about them being applied and may prevent any aggression when the person has to be removed from the cruiser or when the handcuffs are removed. There have been some liability questions over kneeling on a prone subject when applying handcuffs. Therefore, officers should be conversant with departmental use of force policy on this matter.

Earlier, I mentioned the tactical reason for making sure a seat belt is used on a detainee placed in a cruiser. From a civil litigation avoidance perspective, and as a mark of a professional, it should be done to avoid injuries to a prisoner if the driver has to stop quickly or is involved in an accident on the way to the station. Also, officers should control the detainee's head when putting then into the cruiser so that they do not injure themselves when entering.

Other Types of Handcuffs and Restraints

A chapter in itself could be written about other types of restraints. However, I will limit the discussion to a few points. With respect to leg chains, make sure the chain between the legs is short enough to prevent kicking or running. Body chains should fit tightly around the waist, preventing the arms from being used.

Plastic handcuffs can be stored in a hat band and are useful when you have a large number of subjects to arrest (e.g., demonstrations). These can only be used once and require a cutting tool to remove. They are least effective when the palms are placed together, as they can be slipped off unless drawn extremely tight.

With respect to hog-tying, be very careful with this practice. A number of the sudden deaths have resulted from individuals being secured in this position. Officers should make sure that their departmental use of force policy permits this practice and be clear about the situations in which it can be used before employing it.

Duct tape—the criminal's handcuffs—is growing in popularity with the criminal element as a restraint tool. If taken hostage and restrained by duct tape, remember, it can be broken by working your arms clockwise and counterclockwise. If you have some doubt, try it at home.

Equipment Maintenance

Like any piece of equipment, handcuffs can become worn and may need to be replaced. They should be checked periodically for defects such as foreign matter in the handcuff jaws, corrosion, broken, loose, or misaligned parts, key locking requiring undue force, failure to double-lock, handcuff ratchet does not lock automatically with pawl, and ratchet does not rotate freely.

Place your handcuffs in boiling water for 5 to 10 minutes to remove dirt that has collected. After drying, lubricate the handcuffs. Some trainers advocate the use of graphite or silicone, as oil can collect dirt and may also thicken in cold weather, restricting the internal workings of the handcuffs.

One Last Word

The power to restrict a person's movements or liberty should never be taken lightly. Placing handcuffs on a person for no reason may possibly cause that individual to have a lifelong hatred of an officer or the police in general. While you may not care, your brother or sister officer may when they are injured because the citizen you alienated would not assist them when the odds were not in their favor.

Chapter 7

FILIPINO MARTIAL ARTS AND LAW ENFORCEMENT BATON TRAINING

INTRODUCTION

Probably the last thing a senior police official would want a member of his or her staff reading is anything related to Filipino Martial Arts, or FMA. The reason for this is that these arts are commonly misunderstood to be simply "stick and knife fighting." In their place, relying on most of the misinformation circulating about these martial arts, I, too, would probably have nightmarish visions of my officers delivering repeated blows to the head of a poor unsuspecting citizen with the baton. It is this uninformed mind-set that has historically kept police defense tactics instructors from exploring other arts, training methods, and techniques.

In the present world of police defensive tactics training, progressive police trainers have begun to examine various Southeast Asian martial arts techniques to see if they can be adapted for police work. For example, the PPCT leg strike to the lateral femoral nerve of the leg is a variation of the Thai boxing round kick. As well, the PPCT Spontaneous Reactive Knife Self-Defense course is based on the knife-fighting techniques practiced in the FMA of Kali, Arnis de Mano, and Eskrima.

If Filipino knife-fighting techniques can be used by police officers in a defensive tactics capacity, the question then comes to mind, Why can't stick fighting principles or techniques be used in a similar manner for baton training?

Hopefully, this chapter will demonstrate that Filipino stick fighting principles and techniques can, and should, be explored by police trainers for possible inclusion into the defensive tactics curriculum. While the information in this section relates primarily to the use of the straight baton, most of the principles can be adapted to other types of batons (e.g., PR-24, Scepter, ASP, and others).

Stance and Grip

The fighting stance in Filipino stick fighting differs from the usual stance taught to police officers in baton training. In most police training, aside from the Lamb method, the left leg is put forward, the right leg behind, and the baton is held in the right hand. The primary reason for this position is that it keeps the officer's firearm, which for most officers is on the right side, furthest away from the subject. A second reason for this position is that in police training, the rear hand holds the baton so that it can be "loaded" (put in a position to deliver a strike) up on the rear shoulder. From this position, it is felt that a strike can be delivered and the baton can be "reloaded" for a second strike, with less possibility of the baton being seized.

In the FMA, the stick is held in the hand which is on the same side as the lead leg. Filipino stick fighters have found through experience (centuries of battles and full-contact stick fights) that putting the stick in the lead hand affords greater striking distance with the baton. In addition, having the stick in the lead hand allows more flexibility and reach for blocking strikes to the lead leg. The lead leg is a tempting target when it is sticking out that much further than the hand with the baton in it.

While teaching officers to keep the firearm the farthest possible distance away from the subject's grasp is an excellent starting point, both the orthodox police stance and the Filipino stance should be practiced. This is because often an officer will have to deliver a baton strike and may not be in the proper striking position that was taught at the academy. Familiarizing oneself with the Filipino stance and practicing strikes from this position may assist officers in successfully delivering a baton strike if caught in an unfamiliar stance.

One last comment concerning stance. One way of keeping the stick in the lead hand and the firearm a safe distance away is to employ the FMA concept of training both sides of the body. In the FMA, students are taught to use the baton with either hand so that they are never at a disadvantage if the primary striking arm is injured. Right-handed officers may wish to explore this training concept as it will develop skill in their "weak" side.

In the FMA, the stick is held firmly in the hand without the fingers or thumb extended. Any extended digits expands the target areas that can be struck. For example, a stick held in a clenched fist may offer 4-6 inches of target, depending on the size of the hand. Sticking out a finger or thumb while holding the stick will increase that target area by a couple of inches. Anyone who has ever been struck on the thumb or finger by a baton will attest to the difficulty in retaining control of the baton after this occurs. During full-contact stick fighting matches, spectators will often see the combatants spinning the sticks in arcs or circles to distract an opponent or deliver repeated blows. A novice attempting this will find it is easier to do if the stick is held loosely in the hand. Doing this, however, is courting disaster, as a loosely held stick can easily be knocked out of the hand when it is being spun. The last thing any officer would want to have happen when fending off someone with a stick is to have their baton knocked to the ground. Not only does it put one in personal jeopardy, it also causes an escalation to a higher level of the force continuum, such as relying on one's firearm, which may not have been the desired tactical option.

Footwork, Body Rotation, and Distance Evaluation

While empty-hand techniques are usually taught and practiced while on the move, this is usually not the case with police baton training. One of the biggest mistakes in teaching baton techniques is that most instructors teach the strikes from a static standing position, without any footwork. The recruit will usually be rooted to the ground, as if encased in cement, and flail away. In contrast, in the FMA, techniques are taught and practiced from a static position, while moving forward, backward, or sideways, while kneeling or lying down. They are taught in this manner because combat usually is dynamic and fluid, in rare cases will an officer not have to move during a confrontation. Teaching officers to be able to use the baton on the move, even when one has been knocked to the ground, adds realism to training.

In the FMA, the geometric symbol of the triangle is used extensively as a training aid to teach footwork. The purpose of using the triangle is to teach the student to advance and retreat along an angle. For example, imagine a triangle is laid out behind you and you are standing at the point. By stepping back along the side of the triangle toward the base, you have retreated on an angle. This type of defensive footwork is more deceptive than stepping straight back. My FMA instructor uses the adage that when you retreat straight back, even the sightless opponent will have no trouble finding you.

The triangle is also used to teach offensive footwork. Imagine an inverted triangle is laid out before you with the point aimed toward you. By stepping along either side the triangle toward the base, the student learns to advance on an angle. This type of footwork teaches a student how to advance toward an opponent without walking directly into their baton.

One of the ways the FMA teaches the student to add power to baton strikes is to incorporate body rotation or torque. This can be defined simply as putting one's weight behind a strike through body English. Body rotation can be used to add striking power to a forehand strike, a backhand strike, or a chopping strike (called a "rap" in FMA).

I never fail to be amused by the number of officers who, when they are asked to execute a backhand strike, merely swing their arms. To get officers to add body rotation, I usually provide them with a physical skill analogy they can internalize. For example, I tell them to imagine they are swinging a baseball bat but are only holding onto the bat with their front arm. In short order, officers are using body rotation to increase their power. At this point, I also usually emphasize that the head should not be their target of choice in their attempt to hit a home run.

Training with a baton also gives an officer an appreciation of the distance required to execute the technique properly. Instead of just striking the air or a punching bag, the FMA incorporate focused strikes against a moving opponent to train this skill. Traditionally, Filipino masters taught this by having students use rolled-up newspapers. Today, we have the luxury of using padded or soft training weapons which allow officers to train their strikes and also avoid being struck by using the subtleties of distance.

Use of the Alive Hand

The alive hand is not something from a horror movie. In FMA, it refers to the hand that doesn't hold the baton. It is called the alive hand because it comes alive during a confrontation. It can be used to block or deflect an attack, strike an opponent, or trap or grasp limbs. The alive hand can also be used by the officer to stop the swing of his or her baton by intercepting the arm holding the baton during the striking motion.

Many individuals armed with a baton become too focused on the hand that holds the baton, forgetting that they have a number of other personal weapons (i.e., hands, feet, knees, elbows, head) that can be used during a confrontation. This concept of the "one armed" warrior is very prevalent when reacting to an opponent who grasps the officer's baton. Too much time is spent wrestling with the opponent to free the baton, when a simple counterstrike with another limb could be used to nullify this attack.

The late Floro Villabrille was an FMA instructor and a renowned full-contact stick fighter in Hawaii in the 1940s. The majority of his knockouts in the ring came when he struck his opponents with the elbow or fist that was not holding the weapon, because the opponents were too focused on not getting hit with the weapon.

In FMA, the alive hand is trained by placing a weapon in it, usually a dagger, during baton practice. This method of training is referred to as long and short (referring to the long sword and the short dagger) and helps keep the student from focusing only on the use of the baton. For police training purposes, one way to train the alive hand is to train on the heavy punching bag with the baton and to insert empty-hand strikes in between baton strikes.

In police training, one possible example of long and short tactics might be to have the pepper spray canister in one hand and the baton in the other. If the pepper spray does not accomplish the necessary effect, the baton can be used as a backup weapon. This is definitely a preferred tactical option when facing someone with a weapon, if the officer does not feel it is necessary to draw his or her firearm.

With reference to pepper spray, Filipino fighters used a variation of oleoresin capsicum spray of their own to achieve the desired effect. They used to mix cayenne pepper with sand and keep it in a handkerchief to throw it in the face of opponents to blind them. When this homemade pepper spray was not available, Filipino knife fighters would often distract opponents by throwing the scabbard of the knife at their faces before delivering a fatal stab or slash. For the police officer, causing a distraction by tossing an object such as a hat at the face of the subject may create the opening for a successful baton strike.

Flow, Sensitivity, and Reflex Training

One of the key concepts found in FMA is that of the flow. This can be defined as the ability to not rely on a single strike but rather to flow between multiple strikes or flow between attack and defense. Flow practice aids in the development of the ability to turn thinking into action during combat. Developing this attribute allows an individual to do three things almost simultaneously during an encounter: evaluate a scenario (e.g., the status of a threat, whether you have sustained any injuries, the success or failure of your last technique), determine what tactical options are available in terms of offense or defense, then execute these options.

Those who have not practiced flow training can possibly freeze when they are involved in a violent encounter and their mind is focused on evaluating the success or failure of a technique, or evaluating if the blow they have taken has injured them. I have observed that successful fighters often capitalize on that moment when an opponent is in this "evaluation" phase, to launch that follow-up technique that does the real damage. This "freezing" can lead to fatal consequences for the police officer if an opponent retaliates before an alternate defensive or offensive reaction can be thought of and executed. Flow training helps prevent you from being stuck in a "thinking" mode when you should instead be in a "reacting" mode.

A further benefit of flow drills in the FMA is to develop sensitivity and reflexes. Sensitivity in this context can be defined as the ability to recognize what offensive technique your opponent is launching by feeling the pressure he or she is exerting at the initiation stage of the attack. For example, suppose you have seized the wrist of a suspect who is armed with a knife—not the best technique, but one that sometimes happens in a real encounter. If the individual starts to push the knife toward your stomach in a stabbing motion, the pressure sensors in you hand will probably alert you to this intention before your eyes see the motion and send the message to your brain.

FMA flow drills use the constant repetitions of some possible alternative techniques or defenses that may be used in a certain portion of an altercation. These attacks and defenses are done alternatively so that both parties work both sets of skills. The patterns are learned, then worked at increasing speeds so that the responses are ingrained into the nervous system. This develops the ability to react without being slowed by the thought process that goes with developing a tactical option.

To ensure you do not get locked into a set pattern of reacting to an attack–which is a surefire recipe for failure, as fights do not follow set patterns–feints, multiple attacks and attacks using the alive hand are built into these drills in a free-form fashion. This develops an individual's ability to react to new stimuli. For a police officer whose slow reflexes or delayed ability to read new stimuli may be fatal, the benefit of this type of training speaks for itself. These drills must be learned by actual practice with a qualified FMA instructor. If one is not available, videotapes can provide some instruction but lack the benefit of hands-on training.

Lastly, any type of weapons training will enhance the officer's unarmed skills. Because a weapon (baton or edged weapon) travels at such a high speed, being able to defend against it will enhance one's abilities to handle a punch or kick which will be travelling much slower.

Strikes, Stroking Patterns, Chokes, Locks, and Disarms

In traditional police baton training, two types of strikes are usually taught. The first is the strike which retracts along the same line as it was delivered, and the second is the power strike which continues straight through the target. In the FMA, a number of strikes are taught: the *watik*, where the strike retracts along the same line as it was delivered; the *loptik*, where the strike continues through the target; and the *redondo*, where the first strike continues through the target in a circular fashion to deliver repetitive blows. In addition, strikes are taught which use the *punyo*, or the butt of the weapon, and blocks, which are, in reality, strikes to the attacking limb, using the center portion of the stick.

In the Philippines, almost every village or town has its own stick-fighting style, however, what is common to most of them is a numbering system for various types of blows. For example, if one is practicing defenses to a downward diagonal strike from right to left (the most common strike delivered by a right-handed person in combat), one would merely have to ask one's training partner to deliver a number one strike. This was developed as a way to save time when training, especially when using multiple strikes.

After the numbering system was learned, stroking patterns which combined attack and defense were taught to neophytes. Unlike police training, where strikes are taught as the only element of baton training, these stroking patterns provide training in striking and defending against various types of blows. Once again, this is a more realistic form of combat training.

Many martial arts teach locking and choking techniques with the baton, and the FMA are no exception. While I teach these techniques to police officers so that they are familiar with them, I personally shy away from advocating their use on the street. Most police services have discouraged the use of chokes with the baton because there is too much chance of fatal consequences when they are used. From a tactical point of view, such techniques are flawed because one cannot ascertain how effective the choke is with a baton, because on cannot feel how an individual is responding to the pressure of the baton. With respect to joint-locking techniques with the baton, I also do not advocate their use because they require complex motor skills that most officers will probably be unable to execute in a violent encounter when under stress. While an impact weapon can be used in a number of ways, for police I usually recommend that they restrict the use of the impact weapon to just that, an "impact weapon."

What I do stress when teaching police officers is the various disarms that are practiced in the FMA. I do this not so that an empty-handed police officer can disarm an individual armed with a stick but so officers can learn to retain their batons by becoming familiar with the myriad of ways their baton can be taken away from them during a confrontation. I find that once they have learned to disarm someone armed with a baton, they do not become overconfident with their batons.

In the FMA, disarms can be techniques to take the weapon out of the hand, or techniques which cause the opponent to drop the weapon due to a lock or wrench to a joint. However, the disarm most prevalent in the FMA is a technique I mentioned in the last chapter called "defanging the snake." Simply put, the easiest way to get someone to drop a baton is to hit them on the hand or arm that is holding that baton, thereby taking the "fang" out of their hands. In the FMA this can be done when armed with a baton or empty handed. This principle can be found in PPCT techniques which teach the striking of the radial nerves in the arms.

During practice of disarming techniques, students of FMA learn that possible disarms appear and disappear in a heartbeat and therefore must be taken advantage of when they present themselves. In addition, students also learn that a disarm is much easier to accomplish when the opponent is thinking about something else–that "something else" is usually the presence of pain that has been introduced somewhere on their body.

In the FMA, hooking and striking techniques using the butt end of the baton (or *punyo*) are an integral part of training. One of the constant debates in FMA circles, however, is how much of the butt end of the weapon should be extended. Some instructors say a fist width, whereas others say the width of two fingers. The latter have concerns that leaving too much of the base end of the baton exposed leaves open the possibility of that section of the stick being used to lock the wrist. This argument has some merit, as one of the easiest ways to disarm an officer with the PR-24 is to lock their wrist using the extended smaller section near the handle.

Warm-Ups

You may be wondering why this chapter is ending with a section on warm-ups when logic would dictate that this should be at the beginning. This is done as a courtesy to the reader. In my personal martial arts library I have hundreds of books and thousands of magazines, with almost every aspect of the martial arts covered, from Arnis de Mano to Zen meditation, from Ju-Jitsu texts written in 1907 by the instructor of President Theodore Roosevelt, to more recent martial arts such as Japanese shootfighting. In reading these texts and hundreds of others, I have found one thing common to almost every martial arts book–the first third of the book is filled with information concerning how to warm up. Not only does this take up a great deal of text space that could be filled with more valuable information but also, in the majority of cases, the information is wrong from an exercise physiology perspective.

Since I am not an exercise physiologist, I would suggest that you seek out specific information from qualified sources on how to warmup and on how to develop your other physical systems: cardiovascular endurance, strength, flexibility, speed, and balance.

What I will offer, however, is a warm-up exercise that has some practical application for combat. In the FMA, there is a technique called *abaniko* or fan. It is a quick flicking or whipping action of the wrist that can deliver a damaging blow when one does not have the time to use arm strength or body torque, or it can be used to deflect an incoming weapon or blow. As a training exercise, it is done to develop flexibility and strength in the wrists and forearms and is a great way to warm them up before stick drills. Simply grasp the baton in the center (when you become more proficient you can hold the baton by the handle) and hold it over your head horizontally. Rotate your wrist to the left and then back to the right a number of times. The *abaniko* can also be practiced when holding the baton straight out in from of you with the shaft pointed upwards. Once again, simply rotate your wrist to the left and right in quick succession.

For those readers who may doubt the effectiveness of this snappy little blow, at one training session taught by my instructor, Guro Dan Inosanto, a misplaced *abaniko* during practice resulted in a six-stitch cut along the eyebrow of the unfortunate recipient. Clearly, police officers would not want something like this to happen when using the baton, however, it is comforting to know that this technique possesses a considerable amount of power if it is ever needed.

Chapter 8

THE CAROTID NECK RESTRAINT
CONTROVERSY

No other police defensive technique is as widely known to the general public as the carotid neck restraint. Through movies and novels dealing with police and high-profile court cases, the public's awareness of, and in some cases outrage to, this technique has been heightened.

The purpose of this chapter is to examine some of the controversies surrounding the use of the carotid neck restraint so that informed judgments can be made with regard to its use. By being able to make informed judgments, improvements can be made, if necessary, to its use which will support the following goals: (a) protect the public from harm; (b) clarify when, and in what situations, the police may use this technique; and (c) protect police officers and their departments from civil liability.

One of the first controversies with regard to the carotid neck restraint is its placement in the "force continuum." The "force continuum" or the "use of force paradigm" is an ascending continuum whereby levels of use of force can be categorized for the officer. The lowest level of the force continuum is the mere presence of a police officer (level 1). This is followed by verbal direction (level 2), unarmed controlling techniques (level 3), the use of chemical agents or impact weapons such as a baton (level 4), and finally, lethal force (level 5). Detractors of the carotid neck restraint say that it should be categorized as a level 5 technique, as it has the potential for lethal force. Advocates of the technique, however, feel that it is a justified weaponless control technique and should be categorized as a level 3 technique.

In an attempt to provide sufficient information for the reader to make an informed judgment with regard to this and other controversies surrounding the carotid neck restraint, a number of subjects will be examined. The difference between a carotid neck restraint and a choke hold will be explained. The physiological aspects of the application of the carotid neck restraint will be examined, as will the different schools of thought with regard to what causes unconsciousness when this technique is applied. Fatal consequences which are possible when the technique is applied will be examined, as well as other inherent dangers. There will also be a critique of the arguments of both the critics and proponents of the carotid neck restraint, as well as a brief examination of some legal issues surrounding the use of this technique. Finally, a draft course curriculum for the teaching of the technique, and draft safeguards for the application of the technique, will be examined.

Definition

A carotid neck restraint is a police defense tactic technique used to restrain violent individuals. It has been called many names: the sleeper hold, the strangle hold, the lateral vascular neck restraint, the upper body control hold, the lateral vascular control, and, erroneously, a choke hold.

With some minor variations, the technique involves the police officer encircling a subject's neck from the rear with his or her arm and applying "pincer" like pressure on the sides of the neck with the arm. The technique is used to control violent individuals and can, if necessary, render them unconscious as an aid to controlling them.

The carotid neck restraint is not a choke hold which impedes the flow of oxygen to the lungs. It is likewise not a choke hold like a "C clamp," which is a squeezing pressure by the hand on the trachea. Also, it is not a choke with a baton. In fact, the carotid neck restraint should not be lumped in at all with the choke hold family, which includes those techniques that affect the flow of oxygen to the lungs. Choke holds have been largely eliminated by progressive police agencies in North America due to the potentially injurious or fatal consequences which may arise when these are applied.

Generally, a choke hold is applied when an officer puts pressure with the forearm against the throat of the suspect. A number of potentially fatal consequences can occur when the officer uses this "bar-arm" choke. A fracture of the hyoid bone, the cricoid cartilage, the thyroid cartilage, or trachea may occur when this technique is used. This may cause swelling of the tissues in the throat area and can cause strangulation of the suspect. In addition to the potentially fatal physical elements of this technique, the "bar-arm" technique also has many flaws from a defensive tactics point of view. For example, when an individual's breathing is restricted, this causes panic as the person feels they are being suffocated. This will cause the suspect to react violently. When the suspect reacts violently, this can lead to the officer using more pressure to apply the technique, and may also result in the individual overpowering the officer. The carotid neck restraint does not theoretically put pressure against the windpipe, therefore, it is a technique which is different from a choke hold.

Historical Background of Carotid Neck Restraint

The carotid neck restraint was developed as a tactic by veteran police officers who were probably influenced by the Japanese martial arts of Judo and Ju-Jitsu and who borrowed it from them. While the technique may have been borrowed from these grappling arts, that is not to say that other Asian martial arts do not have similar techniques. However, as Judo and Ju-Jitsu were the first Asian martial arts to gain popularity in the West, this is the most probable theory for its development.

Physiological Considerations

There are a number of schools of thought theorizing what causes unconsciousness when the carotid neck restraint is applied. Historically, the unconsciousness that resulted after the technique was applied was always explained as the result of loss of oxygenated blood flowing to the brain through pressure on the carotid arteries. However, one school of thought stipulates that when pressure is applied against the carotid sinus, a slowdown of the heartbeat occurs due to the stimulation of various nerves in the brain. This stimulation and slowing of the heartbeat causes a drop in the blood pressure, which deprives the brain of an adequate supply of oxygenated blood. Another school feels that it is not the carotid arteries but other important veins that are really affected in this technique. Yet another school purports that unconsciousness is the result of shock in response to stimulation of the receptive nerve in the carotid sinus.

Dr. James Cooper, a vascular surgeon, who is chief surgeon of De Paul Hospital, feels that the control (i.e., unconsciousness) established by the carotid neck restraint is a combination of four physiological actions: compression of the neck veins, stimulation of the vagus nerve, compression of the carotid arteries, and the valsalva maneuver. The valsalva maneuver is the pressurization of the chest cavity through holding the breath and contracting the diaphragm, both of which result when one is under the physical stress of being the recipient of the technique while in a seated position.

In 1982, Dr. Donald T. Reay, the chief medical examiner in King County, Seattle, Washington, who has written three scientific papers with regard to the use of the carotid neck restraint, conducted a scientific experiment on the physiological aspects of carotid neck restraint, as he could find no studies which assessed the physiological effects of neck holds. The experiment measured blood flow to the head before, during, and after application of the hold through the use of the laser doppler measuring changes in capillary blood flow to the skin of the face, and ultrasonic doppler to evaluate changes in arterial flow in the temporal artery. In his paper "Changes in Carotid Blood Flow Produced by Neck Compression," he concluded that "with an arm and forearm well placed about the neck, a subject can be rendered rapidly unconscious by externally applied common carotid artery compression" (p. 202).

Carotid Neck Restraint's Dangers and Deaths

Is the carotid neck restraint always a "potentially lethal" technique? In another article, "Physiological Effects Resulting from Use of Neck Holds," Dr. Reay states that in his opinion, the carotid neck restraint should be treated as "potentially lethal whenever applied" (p. 15).

The potential dangers associated with carotid neck restraint are examined below, and some of the literature covering custody deaths associated with it will be perused to aid the readers to come to their own conclusions.

Dangers

There are a number of potentially fatal dangers which are possible when the carotid neck restraint technique is applied. These dangers can be broken down into three categories: improper applications, applications on persons with preexisting physical problems, and applications on drugged individuals.

IMPROPER APPLICATIONS. If the carotid neck restraint is improperly applied, it may result in the police officer applying a "bar-arm" choke, which can result in damage to the throat area from pressure by the forearm. Another improper application of the technique is the jerking of the head by the person applying the technique. This may result in damage to the neck area. The third improper application is an application to an individual in a standing position. This results in the individual hanging without support while being held by the arm of the applicator. This can, as well, lead to injury of the neck area.

When the throat of the recipient is pushed too far forward into the V of the arm at the elbow, this might result in damage to the throat area because the muscles of the arm (brachioradialis and biceps muscle) may produce a crushing effect. If the technique is held for too long or applied repeatedly, it may result in permanent brain damage or death, as the brain is deprived of oxygenated blood used to supply the cells. If excessive pressure is applied to the side of the neck, there is a small possibility that the hyoid bone located at the base of the tongue might break. This may well result in asphyxiation of the individual caused by swelling of the tissue in that area. Lastly, if the individual is seated in a leaning position to the rear instead of in an upright position, the neck could be damaged by full compression of the arm.

APPLICATIONS ON PERSONS WITH PREEXISTING PHYSICAL PROBLEMS. In "Death From Law Enforcement Neck Holds," Dr. Reay states that "pre existing natural diseases increases the likelihood of a fatal outcome, even when a hold like the carotid sleeper is applied correctly. Underlying cardiac disease such as coronary artery diseases and cardiac rhythm disorders are particularly vulnerable to reflex carotid sinus stimulation and hypoxia" (p. 256). Hypoxia is a deficiency of oxygen reaching the tissues of the body. Dr. Reay feels that "the incidence of coronary artery disease increase sharply after the age of forty. This group would be particularly vulnerable to carotid sinus stimulation and/or hypoxia which could trigger a fatal heart dysrhythmia. In addition, in a person with arteriolsclerosis of the vessels of the neck, a neck hold could just dislodge arterial sclerotic plaque or cause damage to the vessel wall with resulting thrombotic occlusion" (p. 257).

He further notes that "persons with a history of seizure disorder [such as] epileptics can have seizures promoted or precipitated by violent activity, cerebral ischemia, or hypoxia. Although not necessarily fatal, a grand mal seizure with its violent movement can cause the person to writhe and jerk against the force about his neck, leading to complications" (p. 257). He is also of the opinion that:

> mentally disturbed persons, particularly the manic-depressive psychotics in the manic phase, . . . can be extremely violent with inordinate strength and unpredictable thrashing movement. Because the mentally disturbed cannot appreciate the circumstance, resistance may be great and only intense opposing force would subdue them. A neck hold about such a person will have no direction and may only tighten indiscriminately to occlude the airway as well as the neck vessels (p. 257).

APPLICATIONS ON DRUGGED INDIVIDUALS. According to Dr. Reay, a neck hold applied to persons using street drugs or alcohol can cause hypoxia and death if applied during their violent movements. He maintains that the side effect of many prescription drugs may also predispose their users to cardiac arrhythmia. Two examples of drugs in common use which he feels may well predispose users to cardiac clications from neck holds are various digitalis preparations and tricydic antidepressants (p. 257).

Custody Deaths

Dr. Reay's conclusion in "Death from Law Enforcement Neck Holds" is that the carotid neck restraint hold is a potentially fatal technique under any circumstance and should only be used when there is no alternative. His opinion is that the hold should only be used in those situations when the officer's or another person's life is in immediate danger and when time or circumstances do not allow for other alternatives to be used. He also feels that neck holds must be viewed in the same way as firearms: a fatal outcome being possible each time a neck hold is applied or a firearm drawn. He points out that the neck hold differs from the use of firearms in that its fatal consequences can be totally unpredictable (pp. 257-258). It should be noted, however, that Dr. Reay's study examined only two fatalities. One must question whether two cases are a sufficiently broad enough sample from which conclusive statements can be made.

A further scientific study was conducted by Dr. E. Karl Koiwai, entitled "Deaths Allegedly Caused by the Use of 'Choke Holds' (Shimewaza)." This study looked at 14 deaths where choke holds were applied. Thirteen of those deaths related to police use and one a martial arts use. Injuries were found to the structure of the neck of all individuals studied. Dr. Koiwai concluded that the number of fatalities resulting from the use of choke holds would decrease if various procedures that he suggested with regard to the training of police were implemented.

The physiological effects cited by Dr. Koiwai relate to "choking of the individual." In his paper, he does not specify what kinds of "chokes" were used. As there are many different Judo choke holds, the deaths studied by him may not have been resultant from the use of the carotid neck restraint. I was unable to ascertain which deaths were caused by the carotid neck restraint, as most of the scientific data Dr. Koiwai listed as sources were from the *Bulletin of the Association for Scientific Studies on Judo* from the Kodenkan in Tokyo. These materials were unavailable from either the Canadian National Sports Library or from Judo Canada, the national governing body for Judo in Canada.

Research conducted by Dr. Elizabeth Lapasota, research forensic pathologist at Barnes Hospital and St. Louis city deputy medical examiner, has introduced a counter argument to the listing of neck restraint as the cause of death in custody fatalities. She has raised the possibility that a number of these deaths could be attributed to sudden death occurring through cocaine psychosis and/or sudden psychiatric death such as acute exhaustive mania death syndrome. This theory suggests that death can often occur via cardiac reflex mechanisms unrelated to any injury or method of restraint used. Death is caused by a fatal arrhythmia of the heart developed from extreme mental stress (Siddle and Lapasota pp. 6-25).

Further study of the research conducted by these individuals with regard to custody deaths, which is beyond the scope of this chapter, would be required to adequately fully address this controversy. However, even then, a conclusive answer to the question whether carotid neck restraint holds are always potentially fatal may not be possible. What is possible to determine from the literature is that this factor should be considered in depth by police services when deciding whether this is an appropriate technique for their officers.

Carotid Neck Restraint as a Tool for Police: Arguments Pro and Con

Use on Violent Offenders

Proponents of the carotid neck restraint argue that, in some cases, rendering a person unconscious is the only way to subdue violent offenders. For those individuals who are oblivious to pain, such as those on the street drugs like PCP (where individuals have been known to snap handcuffs), or those who are mentally ill and cannot appreciate pain, or those who are experiencing an adrenaline rush and therefore do not feel pain, the carotid neck restraint offers the best way to control these persons in a humane way without leaving residual damage.

Critics argue that the carotid neck restraint is a potentially lethal technique which can therefore cause residual damage. As well, as indicated by Dr. Reay, the application of this technique on mentally ill people or persons under the influence of drugs can be fatal.

In the Absence of Other Non-Lethal Means

In a Canadian context, proponents of the technique argue that the carotid neck restraint is a useful tool, as not all police in this country are permitted weapons other than their baton or firearm to control individuals. Specifically, chemical agents such as pepper spray or electric stunning weapons, or other items such as pneumatic guns, capture nets, or plastic shields, are not widely used by police officers in Canada.

As well, proponents argue that the use of the carotid neck restraint is useful in those situations where there is not enough space to use a baton or pepper spray, or the use of a firearm might injure the officer, his or her partner, or other citizens.

Critics of the technique argue that police should withdraw from a potentially violent situation until a person, through mediation or discussion, becomes more amenable to being arrested or until barriers (such as plastic shields) can be obtained to assist in making the arrest. The critics suggest that negotiation should be the key rather than unarmed force. A counterargument to this criticism has been a wry observation of a veteran officer who remarked that police could always wait until the potential arrestee "starves to death" before they effect the arrest.

It Is a Technique That Is Highly Scrutinized

Canadian proponents of the carotid neck restraint argue that in Canada, carotid neck restraint is under a high degree of scrutiny due in large part to the problems that have risen in the U.S. with its use. For example, the carotid neck restraint was a topic of discussion at the Canadian Association of Chiefs of Police training meeting in May 1988, as well as the subject of two public hearings by the RCMP Public Complaints Commission. Proponents argue, therefore, that the Canadian experience will not be fraught with the problems faced in the U.S.

Critics of the carotid neck restraint feel that because there is no uniformity across Canada with regard to the training of police in the use of the technique, policy on its use, or safeguards required when the technique is used, Canada will probably encounter the same problems that arose in the U.S. They argue that the arresting of violent individuals is similar in police work around the world.

A Police Tool More Palatable to the Public

Proponents of the carotid neck restraint argue that the use of the carotid neck restraint generates a better public and media reaction than does a situation where an impact weapon or lethal force technique is used. Persons arguing from this point of view would cite the public's outrage to the use of impact weapons in the *Rodney King* case.

Critics of the carotid neck restraint offer three counterarguments to the above-noted proposition:

(1) If a death or serious injury occurs with the carotid neck restraint, they feel there will be a huge public outcry. In Canada, there have been a number of high-profile incidents involving death at police

hands that have led to headlines, public inquiries, criminal trials, and various commission hearings. However, while this argument is usually true with deaths, this may not be the case with regard to serious injuries. There have been some cases in Canada where serious, but not life-threatening, injuries have occurred when police holds have been used and no great public outcry has arisen.

(2) Whenever pressure point control tactics are used against the nerves of the body to remove non-violent demonstrators, the media is quick to highlight the pain registered in the person's face instead of focusing on the fact that there was a lack of further violence or injury.

(3) If the carotid neck restraint was used and scenes of a convulsing arrestee were broadcast to the public, this may well give rise to a great public outcry.

The Potential for a Fatality

Proponents of the technique argue that in the U.S., very few deaths have resulted from thousands of applications. They argue that the potential for death is limited, as deaths occur in a very small percentage of cases where the technique is used.

Critics of the technique argue that perhaps the small percentage of deaths which have resulted when the technique has been applied is due merely to good luck. They argue that one should not be playing roulette every time a technique is applied. If a technique is supposed to be a level 3 technique (unarmed self-defense), then there should not be a potential for death.

A counterargument to these critics is that every time an unarmed technique is used to control an individual, there is a potential for fatal consequences. It can be argued that no technique is totally fail-safe from causing an unanticipated death.

Removing the Carotid Neck Restraint Will Lead to Unrequired Escalations in Force

Proponents of the technique argue that it is better to use a level 3 technique (unarmed control) than a level 4 (impact tool) or a level 5 (firearm) technique and, in conjunction, argue that if the carotid neck restraint is restricted, officers will, with increasing frequency, escalate from a level 3 to a level 4 or 5 technique.

Critics of the technique argue that because it has the possibility of causing death, it is not a level 3 technique but a level 5 technique. As well, critics argue that police officers will not escalate up to level 4 and 5 techniques if more training, practice time, and in service training were allotted to other control tactics.

A counterargument to this criticism is that one cannot always use control techniques due to various factors. For instance, in summer when the weather is hot, the slipperiness of perspiration can make the use of some control techniques impossible. At the other end of this spectrum, during the winter, bulky clothing can render certain pain compliance techniques difficult to apply successfully. It can also be argued that other controlling techniques, such as joint locks, require a great deal of practice before they can be applied effectively by the police officer.

The Carotid Neck Restraint Does Not Always Have to Lead to Unconsciousness

Proponents of the technique argue that by using a three-stage application (simple restraint, arm pressure, arm pressure until unconsciousness) of the technique and verbal commands, the potential for fatal consequences is greatly reduced, as unconsciousness is no longer seen as the goal. Rather, compliance is sought by the police officer, and the offender is given the option to comply to verbal commands or risk unconsciousness.

The critics of this argument say that in a violent situation where there is a great deal of stress, anger, and fear, it is logical that police (as human beings) will have problems de escalating before the carotid-neck restraint comes to fruition (unconsciousness), that being the stage where control is unquestionably attained.

A counterargument to this criticism is that police officers are trained to de-escalate situations and do so every day. Without their demonstrated ability to do so, we would see more injuries and deaths arising from arrests.

Restriction of the Carotid Neck Restraint Will Lead to More Injuries to Officers and Citizens

Proponents of the technique argue that if it is true that the carotid neck restraint has been instrumental in reducing risk and injury to both officers and citizens, then forbidding officers to use the neck restraint will result in greater harm to both.

Critics of this argument would point out that acceptance of the above proposition would depend on whether one accepted the carotid neck restraint as non-lethal and whether the above-noted argument could be proven empirically.

Comparing Judo Chokes and the Carotid Neck Restraint

Proponents of the carotid neck restraint technique often argue that the mechanics of it are identical to sport Judo *Shime-waza* (strangulations) and point out that the latter have been used in thousands of tournaments and millions of times in training halls worldwide over the last 100 years without a single fatality.

Critics of the carotid neck restraint technique say that training hall or tournament applications of the technique differ from a street encounter, which is a highly stressful situation. Advocates of the technique argue that a tournament is also a high-stress situation and that some contests are all-out "wars," as highly stressed as any street fight.

Critics of the carotid neck restraint point out that a tournament cannot compare to a suspect-officer street fight for the following reasons:

(1) Both contestants in a Judo match know that it is a sporting contest. It is not a life-or-death confrontation or one which, if the suspect loses, he or she may end up spending a number of years in prison.

(2) The contest player receiving the technique will not panic when it is applied, as he or she has had it applied on them countless times in the training hall. This cannot be said of an individual on the street who has never felt the technique applied. As well, tournament players receiving the technique can either give up or allow themselves to be rendered unconscious, as they know that the latter will not result in any fatal consequences. This may not be the case for suspects on the street who have everything to lose if they are arrested or feel they are being strangled to death.

(3) The tournament player applying the technique has had more instruction and practice than the average police officer applying the

technique therefore, he or she can apply the technique judiciously, easing off the pressure when unconsciousness sets in.

(4) Contestants in a Judo match are vigorously supervised by one or more officials who can stop the contest at any time, especially when they see unconsciousness set in. During a street confrontation, there will not usually be a referee present.

The controversy over whether the street application of the carotid neck restraint and sport Judo's *Shime-waza* are identical continues without any sign of being resolved.

Legal Considerations

In any civil litigation suit, complainants usually sue the police service and often allege negligence on behalf of the service in not preventing the injury to the plaintiff by adequately training its officers. In addition to police departments, police defensive tactics instructors should also reevaluate teaching the use of the carotid neck restraint, as they well may be named in such suits in the future.

In defending any suit, a police department will generally argue that the officer's conduct is outside the acceptable standard of behavior for a police officer. The officer will argue that his or her conduct has conformed to departmental standards and procedures and is in line with departmental training. In the U.S., courts have held police departments contributorily liable for failing to adequately train their officers.

Every police service should attempt to limit its potential liability for action by its officers. I would suggest that such liability may possibly be limited by ensuring that the departmental training standards for the teaching of this technique focus on preventing injuries to individuals. This might be done by insuring that training is not aimed to meet minimum standards, nor should it be stagnant. It should be reviewed, evaluated, and modified as necessary. The training should be of sufficient length for cadet police officers to properly learn the technique, and in-service training should be available in the form of refresher courses to veteran police officers.

Course Curriculum and Safeguards

The last two sections of this chapter cover a draft course curriculum for teaching the carotid neck restraint and draft safeguards that should be implemented when the technique is used. These sections are a compilation of my thoughts on this issue, a review of the literature in the area, and existing standards from various police services.

Draft Course Curriculum for Teaching the Carotid Neck Restraint

Any course curriculum covering the use of the carotid neck restraint should, in order to prevent injuries to citizens and civil litigation, take the following points into consideration:

• Specify whether this technique is considered a level 3 response (weaponless control) or a level 5 (deadly force) technique on the force continuum by the police service.

• Sufficient time should be devoted to the teaching and practice of this technique. A few hours of practice given only during recruit training can lead to problems with the technique application in the future.

• The course content should cover the following elements:

(a) anatomical structure and weaknesses of the neck and throat area;

(b) physiological effects of the hold when applied;

(c) method of applying the hold, three degrees of control as taught by the Kansas City Police Department;

(d) the duration of hold when applied;

(e) improper method of applying the hold and the resulting dangers;

(f) potential fatal consequences of the hold even when properly applied;

(g) historical information concerning the lawsuits that have resulted from its use, e.g., *Adolph Lyons* case (Los Angeles Police Department);

(h) first aid procedures upon cessation of the hold;

(i) that the hold should not be applied with an impact tool;

(j) why the hold is preferred over the "bar-arm" choke hold or other neck restraints;

(k) proper body positioning during the application of the technique so that the subject's weight is not left hanging to help effect the technique;

(l) the dangers of repeated uses of the hold;

(m) the danger of applying the hold on some individuals, e.g., those with cardiac disorders, hypertension, undeveloped nervous systems, and those using prescription or street drugs;

(n) the effect of adrenaline in both the officer and the subject resulting from high-stress situations that hinder proper application of the technique; and

(o) the effect of ego in hampering the police officer from realizing that the goal of the technique is control of the individual, not his or her unconsciousness.

Draft Safeguards for Application of Carotid Neck Restraint

As indicated above, there should be a focus on the goal of obtaining control when this technique is applied. When the carotid neck restraint is applied, it is not necessary that it be used until the individual is rendered unconscious. What is sought is control of the individual, not incapacitation.

When this technique is applied, departmental policy should state that, as soon as possible, first aid should be given to the individual, and he or she should be transported to a hospital or to a qualified medical practitioner. The emphasis here is on the words "as soon as possible." An officer who has found it necessary to apply a corotoid neck restraint should render first aid to the suspect, if necessary, and transport him or her to a hospital as soon as possible.

Conclusion

I have purposely tried to remain neutral with regard to the controversies surrounding the carotid neck restraint. By playing devil's advocate and trying to put forward the best case for both sides of every argument, I hope that I have provided the reader with an unbiased view of the controversies facing this area of police defence tactics.

Undoubtedly, the carotid neck restraint works. After having applied it on a number of people very much larger and stronger than myself under some pretty stressful situations, I can attest, as can most officers who have applied it on the street, that it works very well. It does, however, possess some great risks when it is applied. These risks should be carefully examined and weighed by every police service that currently uses the carotid neck restraint.

Chapter 9

DEFENSIVE TACTICS AND THE SMALLER OFFICER

The expression "the bigger, the better" refers to the thinking that was behind police officer hirings in bygone days. Police forces (as they were called then) hired their officers based on requirements that they meet certain minimum height requirements. This practice of "hiring by the pound" continued until very recently and is one of the reasons why people of smaller stature could not entertain the possibility of a career in law enforcement. In Canada, officers of smaller stature are now being hired to accommodate hiring practices which allow more women and individuals from some ethnic minorities that are smaller in stature to become police officers. In addition to ensuring that police services are representative of the public they police, this shift in hiring practices gives qualified and dedicated people, regardless of stature, a chance to enter law enforcement.

It was traditionally held that shorter officers would not be as intimidating to criminals and would, therefore, be in more danger and less able to defend themselves. Studies examining the relationship between officer size and assaults have found no evidence that shorter persons attack taller persons or that taller assailants attack shorter police officers. Despite this evidence, there are those inside the police community, the criminal community, and the public at large who continue to believe the myths about the relationship between the size of the officer and their defensive tactics capabilities.

Why does this myth still persist? My personal theory is that people who choose to believe certain things in their childhood still believe them when they become adults. In childhood, when confrontations become physical, and in the absence of one of the children being

91

trained in fighting, the bigger child usually emerges victorious because of superior size and strength. From these early experiences, we carry into adulthood the notion that physical size correlates with an ability to fight.

My life experience, as a smaller-stature person examining this phenomenon, has led me to believe that in adulthood, larger size often does not correlate to great strength or fighting ability. However, since most people believe it does, larger people usually do not have to become physical with anyone. Lest I be accused of being biased by those who are not "vertically challenged," let me point out that this is only a personal observation. One should not be lulled into believing that big people are weak or do not know how to fight. To underestimate anyone can be fatal in law enforcement.

It is immaterial whether smaller-stature officers are less intimidating or have to resort to physical force more often to effect arrests. Even if these myths were true, there is nothing that can be done to change the following realities: police services will continue to hire shorter-stature people as police officers, these officers will continue to make arrests as part of their job, and this will, in a small percentage of cases, require the use of force.

What is relevant for our purposes is to ensure that the smaller-stature officers are supplied with the training and equipment necessary to do the jobs they have been hired to do in a professional manner. It is also relevant that smaller officers recognize that they may come up against individuals who do not think the smaller officer can physically subdue them, and the officers should be prepared for this. In this chapter, I will examine what tactics and techniques the smaller-stature officer can employ to enhance their defensive tactics capabilities for this purpose.

HOW TO AVOID THE "BIG MAN" APPROACH

Most police defense tactics trainers that I have met, with some exceptions, have been very physically imposing people. Some were former professional athletes, some body builders, and all were very much larger than myself. Many of them used what I call the "big man" approach to teaching techniques. In other words, when their technique did not work because it was not a viable fighting alternative in that particular situation or simply because it was a lousy technique, they would make it work through application of brute strength or greater body size.

A smaller officer must be very wary of any instructor with this teaching style. If the smaller officer is faced with a problem in the application of a certain technique that the instructor cannot overcome without using superior strength or size, the smaller officer should question whether this technique has value for them. This is not to say that some techniques do not require strength or that the officer should not try to master the technique. In any physical confrontation, strength is an attribute that should be developed, as should knowledge of different techniques.

The smaller-stature officer should use the Jeet Kune Do concept of "adopting what is useful." What this means is that the smaller officer should seek out, experiment, and adopt those techniques and variations in technique more suitable for their body type. The easiest way to gain this knowledge is to ask the defensive tactics instructor for techniques, or variations of techniques, that are more suited to a smaller-framed individual. Anton Geesink, the former world and Olympic Judo champion from Holland, once explained that it is better to have two or three techniques that are suited to your size and strength than trying to master many that are useless to you.

A second way to gain this knowledge is to seek out smaller instructors or skilled practitioners and ask them how they have become successful in applying defensive tactics techniques. As well, the smaller officer can "mirror" what they do. "Mirroring" is a proven sports psychology technique whereby one tries to emulate the physical actions and mind-set of an individual executing a physical activity. For our purposes, one could watch how a smaller officer executes a perfect takedown, inquire about what he or she is thinking throughout the action, then mimic these steps.

Conversely, the smaller officer can also seek out larger-sized patrol officers, practitioners, or trainers and ask them what smaller subjects have done during an altercation which has made them hard to handle. I suspect that these officers will have things such as "wiriness," surprise, and reliance on street-fighting tactics on their lists. "Wiriness" can comprise some or all of the following elements: strength disproportionate to size, physical endurance, resilience, an ability and willingness to "hang in there," and the ability to use one's smaller size to an advantage when grasped, by wiggling or generally making oneself harder to hang on to.

TRAINING KEYS FOR THE SMALLER OFFICER

During training, I would suggest that smaller officers first learn how to close the distance between themselves and a taller subject while not getting hit by the other person's longer arms and legs. More information on closing this gap is covered in Chapter 5 on joint-locking, pain compliance, and come-alongs. I would also suggest that the smaller officer learn what is termed "in fighting" in boxing and martial arts. This is where blows are thrown and techniques executed when the officer is very close to the subject. When one is very close to a taller person, the advantage of their longer arms and legs is nullified, while an advantage may be gained by the combatant with superior technique. I stress that this advantage may be gained, because if the opponent is very strong, grappling range may be the last place to put yourself. In such a case, escalating up the force continuum to use your impact weapon would be suggested.

Some people have never hit a larger person out of anger or been hit by a bigger person in their life. These people, after they have received the basics in kicking, punching and defense, should don protective padding and experience some full-contact sparring. This process, while giving them a healthy respect for the reason to avoid being hit, may increase their confidence by showing them that bigger people are not invincible. It will also show them how durable their own bodies can be. Further information on this type of training can be found in Appendix A which details the use of the FIST Police Suit.

Any person seeking to become proficient in defensive tactics should stress the development of all attributes mentioned in Chapter 1 on martial arts training. However, the smaller officer should also strive to develop those needed to overcome a size disparity. For example, if grip strength is required so that the baton can be retained or for grappling, then this should be developed. If the officer requires striking power, then this should be developed. Lastly, smaller officers should strive to develop that "wiriness" mentioned previously and also the ability to kick into their survival instinct mind-set of controlled aggressive fury which will not allow them to lose the fight.

One skill I believe that smaller officers should develop is the ability to pass what I call the "pitbull test." Pitbulls or any other type of fighting dog will often best other larger breeds of dogs during a fight because of both their tenacity and their ability not to be shaken off when they have clamped down their jaws onto the other dog. How does this apply to smaller stature officers? As mentioned earlier, one of the safest places to be when confronted by a taller individual who is a superior puncher or kicker is right on top of them, and not trading blows at arm's length.

Oftentimes, however, when a smaller-stature person latches onto someone bigger, they end up getting thrown off. To avoid this, the smaller officer should practice grabbing hold of and trying to take down a larger individual who is trying to shake them off. Not being shaken off is a pass of the "pitbull test." Picking yourself off the floor if shaken off, and getting back into the fray without hesitation, also earns an honorable mention. While being tossed around like a rag doll is not the ideal situation during an altercation, it is one the smaller officer can end up in. And, it beats trying to trade punches with someone who has 10 or 12 inches of reach on you.

TACTICS AND TECHNIQUES FOR THE STREET

Verbal Skills

Growing up untrained, smaller people have probably had to rely on their verbal skills to avoid "duking it out" with larger kids. There is no reason why these skills cannot be used to talk people into allowing themselves to be arrested, handcuffed, and transported to the station in a peaceful fashion. As I have said, compliance is the easiest way to effect an arrest and is what every officer should strive for, regardless of their size.

Speed and Agility

Sometimes, compliance is not always possible. At these times, smaller officers should use what natural abilities they have been graced with. While not always true, most smaller people can move more quickly than larger people. Consequently, the smaller officer should use greater speed to either distract the subject or strike a blow, if this is required, before the larger individual can react.

In addition to speed, most smaller-stature people are "blessed" with shin and forearm bones that are closer to the surface. The former are great for strikes to the lateral femoral and common peroneal nerves of the thigh, and the latter are great for strikes to the radial nerves of the forearm or the brachial plexus nerves along the side of the neck. In addition, skinny forearms are ideal for creating pain to the tricep muscle insertion into the elbow by grinding during the application of any type of arm-bar hold.

Target Selection

While technique cannot always overcome a size and/or strength disparity between the smaller officer and the larger subject, some parts of the body are vulnerable on persons of any size (e.g., eyes, throat, eardrums, genitals, and knees). Because of their vulnerability, these targets should only be attacked if the officer or another person is in jeopardy for their lives or are risking serious injury.

Equipment

The development of oleoresin capsicum (pepper spray), and other weaponry such as the electric shocking weapons, pneumatic tube guns, and capture nets, have eliminated some requirement for superior size, strength, or technical ability. However, the smaller officer should never neglect training his or her unarmed defensive tactics or rely solely on weaponry. These pieces of equipment are only of value if they can be brought into play during an altercation.

One piece of police equipment was specifically designed for use by smaller officers. The Algonquin College Sure Grip Scepter Baton was invented by one of my instructors, Professor Georges Sylvain, when a number of his students voiced their concerns that they would not feel comfortable using their batons on the street, as they were too bulky and could be taken away from them. Professor Sylvain created the Scepter, which has a shovel-like handle and is much lighter, to address these concerns. He has found in testing this baton that smaller officers can be dragged around by it without losing their grip. The Scepter has gained acceptance as the baton for a number of police services across North America.

CONCLUSION

The unfounded prejudice that smaller-stature officers of either sex do not possess the physical characteristics necessary to be effective during a physical confrontation may prevail. As is the case with officers from various minority groups who have become police officers, the best way to disprove an erroneous belief about one's abilities is to demonstrate to fellow officers that you are a capable individual. For the smaller-stature officer, this may be achieved by learning and practicing how to effectively utilize defensive tactics and by displaying the courage to back up your colleagues during a physical confrontation.

Chapter 10

SPORTS VISION TRAINING FOR DEFENSIVE TACTICS

INTRODUCTION

Every person or police officer I ever trained probably looked into martial arts or police defense tactics because he or she was looking for an edge, something that would give them the upper hand to emerge unscathed from an altercation. As an instructor, I always felt that it was my duty to search out that edge for my students. It is with that goal that I became interested in scientific techniques that would improve the speed and reaction time of my students. I read about race car drivers practicing video games while riding exercise bikes to enhance their reflexes under conditions which simulate the fatigue of a race. I viewed videotapes on how to develop speed. However, I felt that if I was to make any progress in this quest, I should heed my own advice and seek out an expert in the field. Luckily, while watching television one evening, I learned that optometrist Dr. John Granda and his Sports Vision Clinic were located a short distance from where I lived.

Could sports vision training be that edge that police officers might be looking for? I decided to approach Dr. Granda to see if his sports training methods had a defense tactics application. To be useful and something that I would recommend, this type of training would have to be transferable to defensive tactics. For police officers to invest the time and energy in developing their vision skills, this type of training had to be useful for more applications than hitting a home run at the annual detachment picnic.

PREVIOUS KNOWLEDGE OF VISION TRAINING

Prior to meeting with Dr. Granada, I had limited knowledge about sports vision training. I knew from martial arts that everyone has a strong negative reaction to anyone putting fingers close to their eyes. The quickest way to cause a reaction in someone is to flick your fingers close to his or her eyes. Instinctively, the person will throw their head back to protect their eyes. I also knew that getting a finger poked into your eyes hurts like hell and impairs your vision for some time.

During the course of my martial arts training, I have practiced under poor vision or no vision (blindfolded) conditions to develop my techniques and other senses so that I would not have to rely on my vision. This is an excellent training principle to work into your training regime, as most arrests that a police officer makes will probably be under less than ideal lighting conditions.

From my training in the FMA, I knew that when dealing with knife attacks, the pupil is always taught to use their peripheral vision to look out for the alive hand (the empty hand not carrying the blade). An unseen blow by the empty hand when one's vision is focused on the weapon can have disastrous results. Conversely, students of these arts are also taught to watch out for a hidden weapon which might come into play during an unarmed encounter.

From boxing, I knew one of the golden rules that boxing trainers live by: "The punch that knocks you out is the one that you don't see coming." Knockouts can occur when a fighter does not have that microsecond to prepare for the impact of an incoming blow. In other sports, such as football and hockey, this phenomenon is known as "getting your bell rung" when you are hit from the blind side.

As indicated in Chapter 5, I train police officers to use "tactical vision" when closing the gap between themselves and a subject. Tactical vision can be defined as focusing one's gaze on the center of the chest so that your peripheral vision can observe movements of both the hands and the feet. Looking solely into someone's eyes leaves the officer vulnerable to a low-line attack.

Lastly, one of my instructors, a former Korean war veteran and California police officer, the late Bert Poe, once taught me to close one eye for a period of time before entering a darkened room, as this would help my vision adjust more quickly to the darkness. I can attest to the value of this technique, and as it has prevented me from tripping over articles on the floor when entering dark rooms.

VISUAL SKILLS AND THEIR RELATIONSHIP TO POLICE WORK

Dr. John Granda has worked with Formula 1600 and 2000 race car drivers, motorcycle riders, competitive pistol and shotgun shooters and teams, downhill skiers, hockey and baseball players, to improve their sports vision skills. More importantly for my purposes, he has an ongoing friendship with a number of patrol and elite unit police officers.

The first time that we met, we discussed the police practice of hiring officers based on the 20/20 vision test. He assured me that after the interview, 20/20 vision would mean nothing. He was right. As a way of introducing me to the various elements of vision, he showed me how this test is conducted. Quite simply, if one can read a specific size letter or number from 20 feet, one has 20/20 vision.

Dr. Granda then proceeded to put a number of filters over a projector lens displaying the number to demonstrate that while a person can read the numbers at that distance, the numbers might be less than clear because the person lacks contrast sensitivity. How does contrast sensitivity apply to police work? Imagine seeing a suspect at 20 feet away in dark lighting conditions, wearing black clothes and black gloves, carrying a small black handgun in the hand against his or her chest. Would you prefer to have 20/20 vision that would allow you to read the black and white eye chart or the contrast sensitivity to spot that pistol? Hopefully, you are now beginning to question your preconceptions of vision as I did.

Dr. Granda detailed 15 various visual skills and how these can be optimized either by training with specialized equipment or through easy exercises which can be performed daily. I have outlined these skills below. Along with Dr. Granda's definitions and information on how these skills can be trained, I have tried to provide specific examples related to police defensive tactics or general police work.

Static Visual Acuity

This is defined as your ability to resolve detail when both you and the target are stationary. This function may be improved with the appropriate spectacle lenses or contact lenses. A simple police example is how well you sight the target on the shooting range.

Dynamic Visual Acuity

This is defined as your ability to resolve detail when either you, the target, or both are in motion. This function may be improved by optimizing the static visual acuity and also by participating in the appropriate vision training regime.

Such training would consist of trying to read license plates of approaching cars or road signs just before you pass them while on patrol. Another training exercise you can try at home is to scroll down the screen of your home computer while you try to read the contents. If you don't own a computer, try reading the running credits at the end of a television show or a movie as they scroll up the screen.

A police defensive tactics example of how this skill can be used is how well you sight a target while on the move on a combat or fun house range.

Contrast Sensitivity

This is defined as your ability to identify an object against its background. For example, it is much easier to see black print on white paper compared to grey print on grey paper; it is more difficult to drive in the fog than on a clear day; it can be very difficult to track a high-fly baseball through a hazy summer sky. This function may be improved through the proper sunglass or shield; the use of the appropriate spectacle lens design, tint, and coating; and the use of the proper contact lens and contact lens solution.

In addition to the police example related to contrast sensitivity previously mentioned, imagine being able to enhance your vision before searching for a suspect in a darkened area or having a tool appropriate for the lighting conditions that would enhance your vision or eliminate glare while on a stakeout waiting for a bank robbery to take place.

Accommodative Facility

This is defined as your ability to quickly focus from far to near and from near to far. This function will naturally reduce with age but can be optimized with vision training.

According to Dr. Granda, you can train this skill in a number of ways. While in the car, focus on fine detail in the instrument panel, then quickly return your focus to an object over 18 feet away. This procedure can be repeated a number of times.

A very practical police defensive tactics application of this skill would be how quickly you could discern whether the driver you have stopped, and whose license you are checking for warrants on your computer screen, is a threat when you look up and see him or her advancing toward the cruiser.

Eye Movements

This is defined as your ability to move either eye smoothly, quick and efficiently. There are two basic eye movements: quick shifts and tracking movements. Both functions may be improved with vision eye training.

Quick shifts can be trained by shifting your eyes quickly–from observing the detail of one object, over to observing the detail of another object positioned off to the side. Repeat back and forth, side to side. The objects can be at different heights or at different distances from you. This is easily done in almost any environment–for example, when you have a moment while doing paperwork at a desk or while in your police car.

Tracking can be trained by following a moving target with your eyes. Stay right on target and don't drift in front or behind the moving object. Common examples are: following the ball or a specific player when you are watching sports, following the tip of a moving windshield wiper, or following moving objects when you are observing or participating in computer games.

One policing example of quick shifts would be your ability to move your eyes back and forth between multiple suspects. An example of tracking would be for the SWAT team sniper who has to follow a potential target in his or her scope. In both examples, good vision can keep you and others alive.

Eye Teaming

This is defined as your ability to coordinate eye movements and to lock both eyes onto the target quickly and efficiently. One way to test this element is to look at a target over 10 feet away. Hold up your index finger so that it is directly underneath your line of sight to the target. If you look at the target, you should see two images of your index finger (double at near). If you switch your focus to your fingertip, you should see two images of the distance target (double at far). There must be no suppression of vision at any distance. This function may be improved with vision training and with corrective lenses if needed. The training would consist of the exercise detailed above.

Avoiding double vision when scanning full field, or avoiding a blind spot caused by suppression of vision, is necessary in police work. Not seeing a subject, or any potential weapons that person may have, can lead to disastrous results.

Depth Perception

This is defined as your ability to judge the true location of an object in space, even with minimal visual clues. This function may be improved by optimizing the eye teaming and also by participating in the appropriate vision training regime.

Such training would consist of the following exercise. Hold a drinking straw in one hand and a pen or pencil in the other. Have the opening of the straw and the pen tip facing each other. Hold them about three feet apart and in one smooth motion, put the pen tip into the straw opening. Next, try this with one eye closed. You should notice the quality of visual information provided when using two eyes rather than one.

The obvious police defensive tactics application of this visual skill is to be able to discern how close or far away a threat is to you. In a bladed or blunt weapon attack, you must be able to judge how much clearance is necessary to avoid being slashed or hit.

Central Visual Recognition

This is defined by your ability to recognize detail in your central field of vision quickly and accurately. This function may be improved with vision training and also by optimizing visual acuity and contrast sensitivity.

One way to train this skill is to place some family photographs face down in front of you. Flip the top picture over and look at it for less than a second before turning it face down. Now try to remember what was in the picture, who was wearing what clothes, and the like.

A second training example can be done while parked in your police cruiser. Close your eyes and then open them for less than a second before closing them again. Now try to recall what you saw. Repeat the procedure and ascertain if anything has changed in your field of view.

A couple of general police work examples of this skill would be your ability to quickly ascertain whether the person you caught a glimpse of was the suspect on your wanted sheets or whether the license plate you quickly saw was on your list of stolen cars. A further example would be your ability to recognize whether any evidence at a particular crime scene you have previously viewed has been taken or moved.

Peripheral Visual Response

This is defined as your ability to respond to peripheral visual stimuli quickly and efficiently. This function can be adversely affected by stress or fatigue, creating a "tunnel vision" condition. It may be improved with vision training.

To train this element, simply look directly at your television set. How much information can you gather in your peripheral vision as you look straight ahead at the screen? One NFL quarterback with great "field sense" used to train his peripheral vision as a boy by trying to read store signs while he looked straight down the street.

One police defensive tactics example would be your ability to see and react to a blow or weapon coming at you from outside your line of sight by a bystander or accomplice of the person with whom you are conducting a field interview. A second example is your ability to perceive a low kick or low knife slash directed at you by the person whose eyes you are looking at to determine if he or she is displaying signs of alcohol impairment.

Officers who have a background in sports requiring good upward vision (e.g., volleyball, badminton) may need this kind of training to ensure that they are not vulnerable to low-line attacks.

Eye-Hand Reaction Times

This is defined as your ability to move your hand quickly in response to a visual stimulus. This function may be improved with training. Such training would consist of working with computerized reflex boards that flash lights randomly to test eye-hand reaction speed. If you do not have the opportunity to work with such specialized equipment, you can simply throw a ball against the wall and catch it with your hand. The closer you get to the wall or the harder you throw it, the more difficult it becomes, because you have less reaction time.

The obvious defensive tactics example is your ability to recognize a threat and respond quickly with an appropriate empty hand or armed response.

Eye-Foot Reaction Times

This is defined as your ability to move your foot quickly in response to a visual stimulus. This function may also be improved with training.

Training to develop this aspect would consist of a variation of the training regime listed above. Simply kick a ball against a wall and kick it on the return. The closer you get to the wall or the harder you kick it, the more difficult it becomes. Another training method would be to use your foot to keep the soccer ball in the air.

One police example would be your ability to hit the brakes during a high-speed pursuit. Another would be your ability to get your feet in motion to body shift away from an attack or to deliver a kick.

Eye-Hand Coordination

This is defined as your ability to perform a task using your hands, based on visual information. This function relies upon the successful teaming of most of the preceding functions if the response is to be quick and accurate. Therefore, this function may be improved with the appropriate vision training regime and related corrective measures.

A fun way to train this aspect is to use a very soft ball and play catch with a training partner or with a "toss-back" net. The fun part is to try it in a darkened room using only the flash of a strobe light to see. This explains the need for a very soft ball. Boxers and other fighters train this aspect by using the speed bag.

The police defensive tactics example would be the same as mentioned in the section on eye-hand reaction times, but would focus more specifically on your ability to bring your firearm into the proper sighting position.

Eye-Body Coordination and Balance

This is defined as your ability to perform a task using your body based on visual information. Vision and balance are very closely linked, and again, this function relies on the successful teaming of most of the preceding functions. Therefore, it may be improved with the appropriate vision training regime and related corrective measures.

A simple way to train this aspect is to try walking, heel to toe, a two by four plank in stocking feet. While this may be simple enough under normal circumstances, try doing it with your eyes closed.

A humorous police defensive tactics example of using eye-body coordination and balance to your advantage in the field was provided by a member of the Edmonton Police Service Tactical Team. This officer used to destabilize subjects by raising his hand in an upward motion before their eyes (like Curly of the Three Stooges used to do). As funny as this sounds, it worked. According to Dr. Granda, the reason this works is because, as mentioned earlier, we are very protective of our head and face. Also, we are naturally drawn to follow and analyse objects coming close to our face. As the officer raised his hand above the subject's eye level, that person would generally have a natural tendency to follow it up with their eyes which shifted their body weight back onto the heels, making them more vulnerable for a controlling technique.

Being involved in sports and martial arts training are excellent ways to develop eye-hand and eye-body coordination. The higher the level of competition, the greater these skills are developed.

Progressive Pattern Memory

This is defined as your ability to recall a previously observed sequential pattern. This may be important for those individuals who are following a track or a course and must be aware of "the best line" or of hazards that may be built in or which may develop during the event. This function may be improved with training.

Such training can be done through the use of very inexpensive, specialized equipment such as the toy "Simon" where you must recall and reproduce a sequence of flashing lights. A second way to train this aspect is to try and recall, after your drive to work, the different events during your drive and the order in which they happened. The number you can recall and the degree of detail is very important. After driving a new route, see if you can retrace it and the associated details in your memory.

While this ability is needed by skiers and car and motorcycle racers more than police officers, it can be helpful for those who are hidden out of sight while on a stakeout at a previously viewed potential crime scene. When the bust goes down, you certainly do not want to come rushing out from your hiding place and trip over any objects you should have remembered were there.

Anticipation and Timing

This is defined as your ability to anticipate an expected event, timing your response efficiently. This is important for those events that commence with a "standing start" or where an individual must react to a rapidly approaching object. This function can rely upon the successful teaming of many of the preceding functions. Therefore, this function may be improved with the appropriate vision training regime and related corrective measures.

According to Dr. Granda, the old television series "Kung Fu" demonstrated the simplest way to train this element, when the master used to tell his young disciple to "try to snatch the pebble from my hand." A pebble, coin, eraser, or any small non-sharp object is placed in the hand, palm facing up. Have your training partner try to snatch the coin from your hand before you can close your hand to protect it. Do not close your hand until the other person tries to grab the object. Switching roles will train your ability to initiate other quick hand movements like blocks and strikes.

The police defensive tactics example would be to correctly execute a defensive or offensive technique against any attack using proper timing. You have to correctly time a block or evasive move for it to be successful. The same applies to a counterstrike or the stop-hit, as described in Chapter 1.

APPLICATION FOR THE OLDER OFFICER

As someone in my fifth decade and who yearns for those bygone days when I could outrun the linemen on my high school football team backwards while they ran straight ahead, I asked Dr. Granda about the application of this type of training for the older officer. Dr. Granda indicated that while the speed by which one can initiate a movement may slow down with age, reaction time (e.g., the time needed to get out of the way of that sucker punch) can be improved with sports vision training.

CONCLUSION

After having had my sports vision skills tested by both Dr. Granda's specialized equipment and the exercises provided in this chapter, I have come to the conclusion that sports vision training has a place in police defensive tactics training. It does provide an edge that can be used by most police officers in defensive tactics. That edge might simply be the ability to avoid being injured by a surprise attack, but in a job where this edge may enable you to get home safely at night, it's a pretty good one to have. For specialized testing and training, readers are encouraged to contact Dr. John C. Granda at Sports Vision Stittsville, Professional Sports Vision Services, 1553 Main Street, Stittsville, Ontario, Canada, K2S 1A9 (telephone 613-836-2032).

Appendix A

THE FIST™ POLICE SUIT

The FIST Police Suit is, simply put, a "suit of armor." It is a one-piece suit consisting of 12 protective pads that cover the body like a medieval suit of armor, protecting the wearer from being injured by blows. The blows they protect from, however, are not those delivered on the battlefield or the street, but in the gymnasium during defense tactics and baton practice.

History of Modern Protective Training Equipment

While boxing headgear, gloves and various types of protective padding have been around for many years, during the early 1970s, protective training equipment used for combative sports became immensely popular and a number of products were marketed. Together with the success of these products also came a number of criticisms.

Protective training equipment was often derided for giving the user a false sense of security, leading to sloppy blocking or other defensive maneuvers. The reason for this, it was argued, was that the fear of being hit in training had been removed. The critics felt that when users of this equipment were involved in a real confrontation on the street without protective padding, they would be in for a rude awakening when hit by an armed or unarmed aggressor. As the organizer of one full-contact, no protective equipment tournament of that era quipped, "Real men don't wear marshmallows" when they fight. In addition, the popularity of full-contact, no protective equipment extreme fighting martial arts tournaments continues to this day, as does the criticism of protective training equipment.

While any piece of training equipment should be evaluated for possible negative side effects, the type of "hard-core" mind-set manifested by critics of protective equipment should not be at the forefront of modern training approaches for police officers. In much the same way that not every martial arts student will go through the gruelling training necessary to become a full-contact fighter, not every police officer has to endure painful training sessions to be tactically effective on the street. Or, put another way, you don't have to get hit by a bullet to know it will injure or kill you.

Traditional martial artists have also criticized the use of protective padding because they feel it does not force the student to learn to prevent injuries by controlling his or her armed or unarmed strikes. Traditionalists feel that this lack of control, or "focus" as it is often referred to, leads to inferior technique.

While traditional martial arts free sparring without protective equipment is a valuable training tool, it can, however, often result in a game of tag for the highly trained or, worse yet, lead to injuries when practiced by the less skilled. Moreover, while some police officers have the desire and time to learn a martial art and develop this "focus," most recruits and serving officers' exposure and practice of defensive tactics and baton skills are limited to the time they spend at the academy or during in-service refresher courses.

There is, therefore, a niche for the use of protective padding in the training of police officers, and the FIST Police Suit fills it. It provides an injury-free tool that can aid police officers in learning combative skills in a more realistic manner in the short period of time they are exposed to them.

Firsthand Experience

Over the past 20 years, in order to practice unarmed and baton techniques at full power, I have experimented with protective equipment from a variety of sports. At various times, I have used equipment from such sports as baseball, football, racquet sports, Kendo (Japanese fencing), and boxing. The problem with these articles of equipment was that the density of it often varied (e.g., thickness of padding) as did the composition (e.g., rubber, hard plastic shell) and they were designed for other sports purposes.

During the early 1990s, various martial artists and police trainers commented that they found FIST equipment to be an excellent training tool to teach their students, as well as one which might address the problems encountered with using other types of equipment.

I first used the FIST equipment while teaching a female self-defense class and found that it allowed the students the opportunity to practice their strikes progressively on a stationary, stalking or fighting attacker.

Why the FIST Police Suit Is Innovative

To quote the late Bruce Lee, "boards don't hit back." For our purposes, add heavy bags and kicking shields to this adage. This means that any device upon which you practice full-contact strikes (empty-handed or not) is limited as a practice tool if your training partner merely holds it steady while receiving those strikes.

To improve one's combative skills requires, in addition to practicing striking on non-responsive objects, learning to control distance. Controlling distance is the ability to close the distance between you and an opponent, evade being hit, block and deliver an offensive technique and either control an opponent or retreat unharmed. Devices which will help you master proper distance control, while practicing full-power unarmed defensive tactics or baton strikes without hurting your training partner, are therefore essential.

Controlling distance through the use of non-stationary impact-absorbing training devices is the theory behind the use of such things as boxing's focus mitts and Thai boxing's pads (densely padded arm shields that are used much like focus mitts by a boxing trainer). These training devices offer targets for the student to hit while the trainer moves around, constantly causing the student to calculate proper distancing. Footwork is used to re-adjust defensive or offensive positions.

The problem with the use of focus mitts and Thai pads as training tools is that they rely on the trainer's ability to position them as targets and speed in repositioning them to receive multiple hits. Anyone who has used these training devices has probably been inadvertently hit when a strike either misses the target or the holder/hitter miscues.

The FIST Police Suit allows students to sharpen their skills while eliminating the possibility of the trainer being hurt or being too slow. The pads covering the body act as both targets for the student and protection for the trainer.

Evaluation of the FIST Equipment

The FIST Police Suit was field tested by me using the following individuals: law enforcement defense tactics trainers, military special forces personnel and trainers, martial artists, barroom bouncers, weight lifters, body builders, and untrained volunteers (recreational hockey and volleyball players).

The evaluators were of both sexes and of differing heights, weights and builds. The evaluators received/struck light-, medium- and full-contact blows to various parts of the suit and were asked to provide verbal feedback, both during and after testing in regard to the factors listed below.

Factors Considered During Evaluation

Safety

What is considered here is the correlation between safety (preventing possible injury) versus reality (does the wearer feel some pain and, consequently, try to avoid being hit?). If the equipment does not provide an element of reality, then the student could possibly become overconfident. However, no professional trainer should use equipment which exposes a student to possible injury sustained due to the negligence of the instructor during training. With any type of combatives practice, safety and common sense should be paramount.

It is an undisputed fact that the application of fist or foot to the human body produces varying degrees of pain. The more padding one covers the body with, the more this type of pain can be eliminated. However, with more padding, the less agile the wearer is and his or her offensive and defensive skills are concomitantly reduced.

In a perfect world, a suit could be produced which would allow the wearer to be pain free while at the same time able to move freely. We have not yet reached that point. The FIST Police Suit, however, brings us closer to this goal.

The FIST Police Suit provides covering for the head, chest, back, groin, buttocks, legs, arms and shoulders as in similarly padded suits offered by other companies. Not having tested these, no comment can be made on how they would test in the factors utilized in this evaluation.

The chest protector offered the maximum amount of protection due to its double layer of padding. None of the armed/unarmed strikes tested caused any sort of discomfort. Wall-stunning techniques (e.g., bumping an adversary into an immovable surface to cause disorientation) were practiced and the back and chest protectors were found to be more than adequate.

The padding over the floating rib area and groin was insufficient to cushion full power blows, but it was agreed that more padding would inhibit the mobility or striking ability of the attacker. As well, the arm pads, when used defensively by the attacker, were able to absorb the body blows aimed at the ribs. A special heavy-duty groin protector is available from FIST but was not tested.

At my request, FIST did produce some custom-made additions to the thigh pads so that full-power round kicks from Thai boxing students (considered the most powerful kicks in the martial arts) could be evaluated. It was agreed by the evaluators that the additions would be necessary to cushion kicks inflicted on a stationary target by a highly trained individual.

On a moving target, it was felt that a single layer of padding would be sufficient, providing the leg receiving the kick was not supporting the full body weight of the evaluator at the time of impact.

There was unanimous concern voiced by the evaluators about the FIST Police Suit helmet. Their main criticism was that there is insufficient padding in the eyebrow and temple regions or that the padding used was not dense enough to provide adequate protection from heavier blows. It was also felt that it could not be fastened tight enough, as it moved while grappling and had to be readjusted.

The helmet also comes with a built-in plastic visor which provides for an unobstructed view during training. It can be used in varying light level training conditions and does not impair peripheral vision. The evaluators found that the visor was subject to some fogging, even though there are perforations in the plastic to prevent this. This problem can be easily remedied by applying a coating of anti-fogging liquid which is commercially available for scuba diving masks.

When using the police suit helmet to practice responses to attacks against the head, I had some initial concerns about the visor shattering when hit. This concern was also expressed by some of the other evaluators. As the visor does not bear either a U.S. or Canadian Safety Standards seal similar to that found on hockey helmet visors, none of the volunteers were asked to offer their heads as a target for full-force baton and training knife strikes.

The lack of a safety seal was brought to the attention of the manufacturer, along with a suggestion that each suit might come with literature indicating what types of techniques are inappropriate or potentially injurious. The company was open to this idea, and this type of literature may be added in the future. However, the criticisms mentioned about the helmet should not dissuade potential users. The helmet can provide relatively pain-free protection for unarmed, full-power strikes, and it should be remembered that during combatives practice, the head should never be a primary target for the police officer's response to aggression, as the potential for fatal consequences is far too great.

Fit, Comfort and Ease of Movement

The FIST Police Suit takes a few minutes to put on with the help of an assistant to fasten the straps. Therefore, if only one suit is available, it is suggested that one person be designated as the wearer for a specific length of time so that training time is not wasted "suiting up." The pads themselves hang by a series of straps which prevent them from moving too much during practice.

While the FIST Police Suit offers some understandable encumbrances to natural movement, it is not too inhibiting, nor does it make you feel claustrophobic or that you are moving around like a space age version of *The Mummy*. The suit is surprisingly light and comfortable but does add an extra 15 pounds which will cause the wearer to work up a sweat during a vigorous training session. The chest protector can be adjusted so that it does not inhibit breathing in any way.

The FIST Police Suit can be worn by persons of differing heights and weights. However, certain movements (especially kicks) by shorter officers may be inhibited due to the close proximity of some of the various pads. Conversely, while extremely tall people may be able to kick more freely with the equipment, some portions of various parts of their bodies may not be totally covered due to the length of certain pads. This is not an insurmountable problem, as vital areas of the body are usually covered.

Adaptability and Applicability to Ground Fighting

The FIST Police Suit is highly adaptable. Different parts of the equipment (including additional pieces to cover the hands and feet which can also be purchased) can be used independent of the others, enabling the student to focus on a particular defensive response being trained. For example, if you are practicing baton strike to the common peroneal nerve in the thigh, the individual acting as the attacker only has to don the thigh pads.

The FIST Police Suit can be used in baton training (e.g., straight baton, PR-24, Scepter, ASP/PPCT/Monadnock collapsibles), knife defense, handcuff and weapon retention training. It should be remembered, however, that with any kind of weapons training, care should always be given to safety. Baton strikes should be limited to targets deemed acceptable by the police service's directives and force continuum.

The FIST Police Suit is not limited to the training of strikes from a standing position but can be used to train strikes delivered from the ground or while grappling with an adversary. Care should be exercised when practicing joint-locking or pain compliance techniques on a padded attacker. The padding may inhibit proper application of the technique and give rise to possible injury.

Durability

The FIST Police Suit is made of durable polymer and is covered by a layer of 500 denier cordura nylon. Martial artist Ralph Mroz conducted testing of the durability of the suit. He put the shin guard (the thinnest part) over a braced four-inch piece of wood (the approximate shape of the average human calf) and pounded it with a police baton 1,000 times. The guard showed no signs of wear and when used by him again in sparring, the difference between it and the other shin guard was not noticeable.

The cordura nylon covering is a definite advantage that the FIST Police Suit offers over other types of protective suits. These latter suits, where the protective material is not covered, are subject to cuts and tears and have to be repaired or will wear out quickly. That having been said, it is suggested that a layer of light clothing be worn between the skin and the FIST Police Suit to prevent any abrasions or irritations caused by friction during use.

Portability

The FIST Police Suit comes with a convenient carrying bag with straps as part of the purchase price. The carry bag is extremely useful, as finding a bag suited for specific pieces of equipment is always difficult. Moreover, using other sporting equipment bags is frustrating as most are not large enough to store all of the equipment and this results in pieces being lost. Putting the unit in the bag is, however, a challenging experience the first couple of times, until the user becomes familiar with it.

Cleanliness

Machine washing the FIST Police Suit is not recommended. In view of the size of the various pieces, this would also be impractical. The manufacturer suggests that it be cleaned with a standard household spray cleaner and a cloth. The wearing of a layer of light clothing (as suggested above) will also help absorb the perspiration produced by wearing the suit.

Price

The FIST Police Suit retails for about $760 U.S. and can be obtained from FIST, Inc. by writing to the company at 35 York Street, Brooklyn, New York, 11201 (telephone 718-643-3478 or 1-800-443-3478, fax 718-858-6878).

CONCLUSION

The FIST Police Suit is training equipment for the modern police service. It provides an opportunity for service members to practice appropriate defensive tactics under conditions more realistic than merely striking out in the air or hitting an immovable heavy bag or trainer's focus mitts. It also allows them the opportunity to feel some of the pain associated with the impact of blows—the usual by-product of a real-life physical confrontation—without suffering any residual injuries.

In addition to the physical advantages of training with protective equipment, training with the FIST Police Suit also offers a unique psychological training advantage. Perhaps the worst fear of anyone who practices defensive tactics is to encounter that individual upon whom empty-hand techniques have no effect. This is of greater concern to the police officer who may encounter such a person who may be under the influence of drugs or alcohol. Unlike most others in society, the police officer cannot run away in such a situation and has to make a split-second decision whether to escalate to higher levels of force (e.g., impact weapons, irritant sprays, carotid neck restraint or firearms) or not. The FIST Police Suit offers patrol officers the chance to work through this scenario in the gym, where they can practice alternative controlling techniques without panicking, and not in the street where often there are no second chances to get things right.

In the limited amount of time allocated to defensive tactics training during recruit or in-service training, the FIST Police Suit is a tool which offers a good return for the investment. Practice with the FIST Police Suit should sharpen the defensive tactics skills of police officers, which may in turn assist them in defending themselves or in making arrests where an appropriate and judicious amount of force is necessary.

Appendix B

FACING THE BLADE: UNARMED SELF-DEFENCE AGAINST THE KNIFE

This appendix reviews the training video, *Facing the Blade: Unarmed Self-Defence Against the Knife*, produced by Jeff Kunz and Ralph Mroz. This 80-minute VHS video is available from Defensive Research, 64 Cleveland St., Greenfield, MA 01301.

INTRODUCTION

Professional martial arts instructors and police self-defense trainers are much like individuals in any other walk of life in at least one respect. That is, you can rarely find two who will agree that a certain course of action is the correct manner in which to proceed.

For example, if 50 instructors or trainers viewed the Kunz and Mroz videotape, at least half of them would offer a "better" method of dealing with the knife when unarmed. What you should know is that the "solutions" proposed by these instructors and those of Kunz and Mroz are both correct.

You may be asking yourself how all the different solutions can possibly be correct. The short answer is, because none of them are wrong, given the proper context. On any given day, even the most unrealistic techniques may work. Conversely, while some techniques have fewer flaws and are more favorable in most situations, none are without their shortcomings and all have the potential for failure.

What is meant by "context" are a number of factors that need to be more in your favor than in that of your attacker. These factors include, but are not limited to, speed, visual awareness, strength, footing, sobriety, physical conditioning, fear, anger, the ability to withstand pain, and technical skills both you and your attacker possess. Coupled with the elements that define "context" are the technical strengths and weaknesses of the particular technique being applied.

The challenge of becoming adept at self-defense is to work through the myriad of techniques to find those suited to your physical abilities, discerning those which may work a greater percentage of the time, and being able to adapt these techniques to meet different situations and opponents. Examination of the Kunz and Mroz videotape is a worthwhile step in this exercise of self-discovery.

OVERVIEW OF THE VIDEO

The video begins with an introductory section describing different types of knife attacks, the speed of attacks, and an examination of attacks with other weapons. This is followed by a section on "knife defense fallacies," covering the myth that attacks will be a single, wide motion slash or stab, and the myth that the attacker will only use his or her knife hand during an attack. The "fallacies" section provides a number of very informative examples of misinformation concerning knife attacks.

Kunz and Mroz then explain their ACDC system of knife self-defense with a visual application of the principles involved and practice drills for each of the elements of the system. Proper body mechanics and the development of the attributes (i.e., qualities possessed by an athlete mentioned in Chapter 1) necessary to defend against an attack are covered.

Finally, Kunz and Mroz summarize the material presented and discuss training tips for safe practice of the system.

The ACDC System

The ACDC system of knife defense was developed by Kunz and Mroz by combining elements of Filipino Martial Arts and the concepts of Jeet Kune Do. The acronym stands for: Avoid, Control, Destroy, and Cover. *Avoid* means to avert a potentially dangerous situation by various means. Life-style changes (e.g., not frequenting the wrong places) may be involved and if an attack occurs, avoiding the initial slash or stab while entering into a proper defensive position. Causing pain to the attacker upon entry is also included in this section. *Control* means to manage the arm with the knife, for a brief period of time, to prevent a renewed attack. Mroz and Kunz point out that the length of time where control is possible may be limited to mere seconds. *Destroy* means to hamper the delivery system of the knife and the attacker. Various types of blows to vulnerable parts of the body, which will dispatch the attacker quickly, are discussed here. Lastly, *Cover* means to seek protection or assistance, recovering the weapon for evidentiary or self-defense purposes, and, most importantly, treating any injuries suffered.

A Training Video for Police

I would be remiss in not pointing out that as an instructional tool for the training of police officers (although Kunz and Mroz preface their video with a disclaimer indicating that it is for "demonstration purposes" only), the video has some significant gaps.

True to its title, the video is almost totally geared toward unarmed hand-to-hand responses to the knife. The video does not provide sufficient information concerning the use of other options available to police officers. The use of other police weapons (i.e., baton, oleoresin capsicum spray, and firearms) is not sufficiently covered, nor is adequate information given regarding the use of improvised weapons and environmental makeshift "shields."

Kunz and Mroz do, however, provide information concerning the distance an attacker armed with a knife can cover in a short period of time. This information is similar to an example given in the video *Surviving Edged Weapons*, a video complete with information on the dangers of knife attacks and the range of options open to police officers.

The ACDC system, however, appears to be an unarmed response system that can be taught relatively quickly to groups which have limited time in which to learn and practice defensive skills. It encompasses a number of gross motor skills which can be easily learned and retained by recruits and veteran officers alike—aspects to consider when evaluating any police self-defense system.

A Self-Defense Video

As an unarmed self-defense tactics video, Kunz and Mroz offer the viewer a great return on the time invested exploring their system. The video contains several physical skill demonstrations and plenty of lecture material. The viewer, therefore, may wish to review the tape in sections to avoid information overload.

The video provides an interesting examination of the flaws found in traditional martial arts techniques when applied against the knife. While other videos have also discussed this material, Shihan Tony Annesi, a guest speaker on the video, provides interesting historical information and variations on the use of the X block (a crossed forearm block), which is still being taught in its traditional form, even though the technique has its flaws.

Annesi demonstrates how this technique was originally intended for defense against the sword in a situation where both hands are holding the weapon. He then demonstrates how the original technique can be modified through the use of nerve strikes for application against knife attacks.

MERITS AND DRAWBACKS

While being billed a "demonstration video," *Facing the Blade* is unlike any other martial arts demonstration an individual will probably ever view. In most martial arts demonstrations, the defensive techniques are usually crisp and impressive. As well, the attackers are usually dispatched without the defender working up a sweat or getting a hair out of place.

As most street patrol officers already know, it doesn't work that way in real life. In actual street confrontations, the techniques used are often sloppy and do not always work. Many of the reasons for this can be traced back to the "intangibles" outlined earlier under the definition of context.

Facing the Blade attempts to realistically portray knife self-defense training. Kunz, Mroz and their assistant perform their techniques at full speed and with maximum power–the result being that the techniques closely resemble how they will actually look given a "real-life" situation. From a production point of view, the video also contains a number of scenes which could have been edited out—some for safety considerations (e.g., potentially dangerous footwork patterns) and others that would have made for a better quality video.

CONCLUSION

Facing the Blade does not contain the definitive answer to the knife attack problem—no video or self-defense system does. Some are better, some are worse, given the proper context. *Facing the Blade* is a worthwhile step in discovering what techniques of self-defense may work for the individual.

As mentioned throughout the book, in Jeet Kune Do there is a concept applied in the consideration of any self-defense technique. That concept is to absorb what is useful to you and conversely to reject what is useless. *Facing the Blade* contains elements you may wish to fit into your self-defense repertoire while discarding those which do not and is, therefore, a worthwhile watch.

BIBLIOGRAPHY

Abbott, Jack Henry. *In the Belly of the Beast: Letters from Prison.* New York: Random House, 1981.

Allen, Bud, and Diana Bosta. *Games Criminals Play: How You Can Profit by Knowing Them.* Susanville: Rae John, 1981.

Ayoob, M. *Fundamentals of Modern Police Impact Weapons.* Concord: Police Bookshelf, 1984.

The Balisong Knife. Perf. Jess Imada. Videotape. Tortoise Video, n.d.

Boulay, John. "Emergency Care for Choke Holds." *Coaching Review.* Coaching Association of Canada, Sept.-Oct. 1986: 55-57.

Braden, Charles E., and James W. Lindell. "Police Neck Restraints: At the Crossroads." *The Police Chief.* Jul. 1982: 53-59.

Campbell, S., G. Cagaanan, and S. Umpad. *Balisong: The Lethal Art of Filipino Knife Fighting.* Boulder: Paladin, 1986.

Christensen, Loren W. "Chokes and Sleepers." *Black Belt Magazine,* Sept. 1981: 40-44.

Creighton, Barry W. "Carotid Restraint: Useful Tool or Deadly Weapon?" *Trial Magazine,* May 1983: 102-106.

Defending Against the Blade. Perf. Peyton Quinn. Videotape. Calibre Press, 1992.

Defensive Edge, Vols. 1 and 2. Perf. Ernie Franco. Videotape. Tortoise Video, 1989.

Diaz-Cobo, Oscar. *Unarmed Against the Knife.* Boulder: Paladin, 1982.

Downey, R., and J. Roth. *Weapon Retention Techniques for Officer Survival.* Springfield, IL: Charles C Thomas, 1981.

Downey, Robert J., and Jorden T. Roth. "The Choke Hold: Asset or Liability?" *Police Product News,* May 1982: 66-68.

Echanis, M. *Knife Fighting, Knife Throwing for Combat.* Burbank: Ohara, 1978.

Echanis, M. *Knife Self-Defence for Combat.* Burbank: Ohara, 1977.

Endow, Ken. "Danger in the Judo Choke?" *Black Belt Magazine,* Mar. 1970: 23-27.

Fabian, Richard L. "Sports Injury to the Larynx and Trachea." *The Physician and Sportsmedicine,* 17.2 (1989): 111-118.

Facing the Blade: Unarmed Self-Defence Against the Knife. Perf. Jeff Kunz and Ralph Mroz. Defensive Research, n.d.

Fairbairn, W.E. *Get Tough.* Boulder: Paladin, 1942.

Filipino Knife Fighting. Perf. Paul Vunak. Panther Productions.

Foo, Gary. *Tactical Communication.* Toronto: Excalibur House, 1995.

127

Fyfe, James J. "The Los Angeles Chokehold Controversy." *Criminal Law Bulletin,* 19.1 (1983): 61-67.

Harstell, L. *Jeet Kune Do: Entering to Trapping to Grappling.* Burbank: Unique Publications, 1984.

Haskew, Mike. "Blades Behind Bars." *Blade Magazine,* Jul.-Aug. 1993: 42-44.

Hawley, Jerry. "Carotid Hold Safe Alternative to Choke Hold Studies Show." *Crime Control Digest,* Nov. 1982: 5-6.

Hosey, Timothy. "Street-Smart Fighting: Putting the Environment on Your Side." *Karate Illustrated* 10.2 (1979): 30.

Hoy, Michael. *Exotic Weapons: An Access Book.* Port Townsend: Loompanics Unlimited, 1982.

Ikai, M., et al. "Physiological Studies on 'Choking' in Judo." *Bulletin of the Association for the Scientific Studies on Judo.* Tokyo: Kodenkan, 1958.

Imada, J. *The Advanced Balisong Manual.* Los Angeles: Know Now, 1986.

Imada, J. *The Balisong Manual.* Los Angeles: Know Now, 1984.

Inosanto, D., G. Foon, and G. Johnson. *The Filipino Martial Arts: As Taught by Dan Inosanto.* Los Angeles: Know Now, 1980.

Jenks, H., and M. Brown. *Bloody Iron.* Cornville: Desert, 1978.

Jenks, Harold J., and Michael H. Brown. *Prison's Bloody Iron.* Cornville: Desert, 1978.

Kali JKD 4. Perf. Ted Lucaylucay. Videotape. I & I Sports Supply, 1982.

Kent, C., and T. Tackett. *Jeet Kune Do Kickboxing.* Los Angeles: Know Now, 1986.

Koiwai, E.K. "Deaths Allegedly Caused by the Use of 'Choke Holds' (Shime-waza)." *Journal of Forensic Sciences,* 32.2 (March 1987): 419-432.

Kornblum, R. "Medical Analysis of Police Chokeholds and General Neck Trauma." *Trauma,* 1 (1986). N. pag.

Kurland, Harvey L. "Mat Dangers: Aikido and Judo Injuries Compared." *Black Belt Magazine,* Mar. 1980: 41+.

Liddy, G. Gordon. *Will.* New York: Dell, 1980.

MacKay, R. *Modern American Fighting Knives.* Burbank: Unique, 1987.

Mashiro, N. *Black Medicine Volume II: Weapons at Hand.* Boulder: Paladin, 1979.

Maynard, R. *Tanto: Japanese Knives and Knife Fighting.* Burbank: Unique, 1986

McGrath, Alice. "Is it True What They Say About Choke Holds?" *The Police Chief* Nov. 1978: 52-55.

Meany, Daniel J., III. "Welcome to Gladiator's School." *Fighting Knives Magazine,* Sept. 1993: 34-39.

Meyer, C. Kenneth, et al. *Ambush-Related Assaults on Police: Violence at the Street Level.* Springfield, IL: Charles C Thomas, Publisher 1986.

Ogawa, S., et al. "Physiological Studies on 'Choking' in Judo." *Bulletin of the Association for Scientific Studies on Judo.* Tokyo: Kodenkan, 1963.

Pearson, Nels P. "Police Choke Holds: The Bottom Line." *Law and Order,* Jan. 1984: 31 33.

Pentecost, Don. *Put 'em Down, Take 'em Out: Knife Fighting Techniques from Folsom Prison.* Boulder: Paladin, 1988.

Reay, Donald T. "Physiological Effects Resulting from Use of Neck Holds." *FBI Law Enforcement Bulletin,* Jul. 1983: 12-15.

Reay, Donald T., and G. Allen Holloway, Jr. "Changes in Carotid Blood Flow Produced by Neck Compression." *The American Journal of Forensic Medicine and Pathology,* 3.3 (1982): 199-202.

Reay, Donald T., and John W. Eisele. "Death From Law Enforcement Neck Holds." *The American Journal of Forensic Medicine and Pathology,* 3.3 (1982): 253-258.

Remsberg, Charles. *The Tactical Edge: Surviving High Risk Patrol.* Northbrook: Calibre, 1986.

Robinson, L., et al. *Public Hearing into the Complaints of Michael and Steven Cooper.* RCMP Public Complaints Commission. Victoria, BC: 1991.

Sanchez, J. *Slash and Thrust.* Boulder: Paladin, 1980.

Sharp, Arthur G. "The Carotid Neck Hold: Myth vs. Reality." *Law and Order,* Mar. 1989: 31-34.

Siddle, Bruce, and James A. Cooper. "Medical Implications of Neck Restraints." *PPCT Defensive Tactics Instructor's Manual.* Millstadt: n.p., 1991. N. pag.

Siddle, Bruce K., and Elizabeth Lapasota. "Deaths in Custody Related to Subject Control Tactics: Use of the Neck Restraint." *PPCT Defensive Tactics Instructor's Manual.* Millstadt: n.p., 1985a: 6-26.

Siddle, Bruce, and Elizabeth Lapasota. "Sudden Death Syndrome." *Police Product News,* Aug. 1985b: 20-23.

Siddle, Bruce, and Vance McLaughlin. "Law Enforcement Custody Deaths." *The Police Chief Magazine,* Aug. 1988, 38-41.

Smith, D. "Report on the Lateral Vascular Neck Restraints." *Carotid Restraint.* Toronto, ON: Bick College, 1992.

Souza, Lawrence J., and Joseph E. Scuro, Jr. "Civil Liability Consequences for Improper Training of Officers." *Law and Order,* Mar. 1983: 35-38.

Steele, D. *Secrets of Modern Knife Fighting.* Arvada: Phoenix, 1975.

Steiner, B. *Close Shaves: The Complete Book of Razor Fighting.* Port Townsend: Loompanics, 1979.

Surviving Edged Weapons. Videotape. Calibre Press, 1988.

Suzuki, K. "Medical Studies on 'Choking' in Judo, With Special Reference to Electroencephalographic Investigation." *Bulletin of the Association for the Scientific Studies on Judo.* Tokyo: Kodenkan, 1958.

Sylvain, Georges J. *The Algonquin College Sure Grip "Scepter" Baton.* Ottawa, ON: Media Algonquin, n.d.

Trevanian. *Shibumi.* New York: Ballentine, 1979.

Younkins, Jerry. "Improvise to Survive." *Warrior's Magazine,* 20 (1985): 24+.

Zeloof, Joe. "Using Tools as Weapons." *Karate Illustrated,* 11.2 (February 1980): 32-34.

INDEX

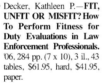